BABIES AND THEIR MOTHERS

D. W. WINNICOTT

Babies and

Edited by
CLARE WINNICOTT
RAY SHEPHERD
MADELEINE DAVIS

A Merloyd Lawrence Book

Classics in Child Development

Their Mothers

Introduction by Benjamin Spock, M.D.

Addison-Wesley Publishing Company, Inc.

READING, MASSACHUSETTS   MENLO PARK, CALIFORNIA

NEW YORK   DON MILLS, ONTARIO   WOKINGHAM, ENGLAND

AMSTERDAM   BONN   SYDNEY   SINGAPORE

TOKYO   MADRID   SAN JUAN

Library of Congress Cataloging-in-Publication Data

Winnicott, D. W. (Donald Woods), 1896–1971.
   Babies and their mothers.

   "A Merloyd Lawrence book."
   Bibliography: p.
   Includes index.
   1. Infants—Care and hygiene—Psychological aspects.
2. Mother and infant.   3. Childbirth—Psychological
aspects.   4. Interpersonal communication.   I. Winnicott,
Clare.   II. Shepherd, Ray.   III. Davis, Madeleine.
IV. Title.
RJ61.W76   1987   155.6'463   86-25887
ISBN 0-201-16516-3
ISBN 0-201-07677-2 (pbk.)

First United States Edition

Introduction copyright © 1987
by Addison-Wesley Publishing Company, Inc.
Jacket design by Laurie Dolphin
Text design by Dede Cummings
Set in 11-pt. Janson by Compset, Inc., Beverly, Massachusetts

CDEFGHIJ-DO-898

Third Printing, July 1988

CONTENTS

INTRODUCTION

by Benjamin Spock, M.D.

I well remember, back in the 1930s when I was starting pediatric practice in New York, my excitement in finding Dr. Winnicott's first book *Disorders of Childhood*. Here were words of wisdom from a psychoanalyst in London who had begun as a pediatrician and therefore had special insights into the mother-infant relationship.

At the time, I was groping and frustrated. During my pediatric residency I had picked up the idea somewhere — certainly not from any of my teachers or colleagues — that I should have some kind of psychological training in order to practice pediatrics in a way that would satisfy mothers, and also to satisfy myself that my advice was sound. (I was of an overly conscientious and teacherish make-up.) Perhaps this idea grew from the feeling that there must be a pleasanter way to raise children than my tyrannical mother's. Though she loved babies and devoted her life exclusively to her six children, she nevertheless oppressed us all with her stern

Victorian morality and left us as adults feeling guilty until proved innocent.

I had written to three professors of pediatrics about psychological training for a pediatrician, but they all replied that there was no such thing. So, following medical tradition, I applied for a psychiatric residency at New York Hospital-Cornell Medical School (a university department of child development might have been more appropriate), where I spent a year caring mainly for schizophrenic and manic-depressive adults. The only usable thing I learned was that the attending staff members who made our case discussions interesting were those trained in psychoanalysis. So I resolved, as I started pediatric practice, to get that training: a personal analysis, five years of evening seminars, analysis of a patient under supervision. (I might, like Winnicott, have moved on to the practice of psychoanalysis had I succeeded in turning my patient into a happy person. I learned a lot but didn't help my patient.)

Psychoanalytic training gave me a sound theoretical framework but no practical advice for anxious mothers worried about thumb sucking, resistance to weaning and toilet training, or feeding and sleep problems. Still feeling unsure and uneasy, I gave the best advice I could think of and then listened attentively to what mothers reported at the next visit — and the next.

After five years of practice I was asked by a publisher to write a book for parents. I said unhesitatingly that I didn't know enough. Five years later came a droll editor from Pocket Books who said the book they wanted didn't have to be very good because, at twenty-five cents a copy, they could sell tens of thousands. That appealed to me both as a do-gooder and as a person afraid to claim too much expertise, and I set to work. The reason these publishers had come to me was not because I was well known — I was utterly un-known except for a small clientele of psychologically minded mothers. The publishers came because their inquiries re-vealed that I was the only pediatrician with any psychiatric and psychoanalytic training.

Even though Winnicott's books and articles were more concerned with meanings than with practical answers for mothers, I had a great interest and trust in them. His psy-choanalytic training and his analytic work with adults, chil-dren, and borderline psychotic patients gave him new, deeper insights into the subtleties of the mother-child rela-tionship and of the stages each was going through. Because of this special expertise, he became one of the major theore-ticians of the British psychoanalytic movement, and most of his publications focused on this subject. For me, he helped to bridge the gap between pediatrics and the dynamics of child development.

This book is composed of talks given by Winnicott, not to psychoanalysts, but to pediatricians, general practitioners, nurses, midwives, nursery school teachers and parents, not only in Britain but in international meetings. A few exam-ples show his focus.

In "The Ordinary Devoted Mother" he expresses his deep faith (which crops up in other talks, too) in the broad capa-bility and correctness of a mother's intuition about what her baby feels and needs, and how this enables the baby's trust to form and his or her increasingly complex development to proceed.

The mother acquires this intuition primarily through her extraordinary capability to identify with her baby. And the baby gets carried along by identifying with her. First the baby assumes that he and his mother are one and the same. Then gradually he senses and asserts his autonomy. The early relationship between mother and baby must not be interfered with by anybody — physicians, nurses, baby nurses in the home, untrained in psychodynamics — for they may undermine the mother's self-confidence and, secondarily, the baby's integrity.

In a radio broadcast to mothers, on whose side he is *always* firmly planted, Winnicott comes back to his emphasis on the great differences between *knowing* and *learning*. A mother knows or soon finds out, by intuition, how to hold and handle a baby so that the baby and she are comfortable and secure. Another example: when an older child gets hurt, climbs in her mother's lap and cries miserably, like an infant, the mother knows, without wondering or asking, that for ten minutes the child must be a baby again and will then revert to her proper age.

Learning from the doctor what vitamins are necessary, and in what dosage, is an entirely different matter. Winnicott says firmly: Don't let the professionals, when they give you information to learn, take away from you your confidence in your natural knowledge.

In "Breast-feeding as Communication" Winnicott first dissociates himself from those who try to *make* mothers breast-feed. (I feel the same way.) The most that doctors and nurses can do is create an atmosphere in which the mother can believe in herself, and then depend on her own intuitive reactions. He speaks approvingly, though, about the taste, smell, and other sensuous experiences of breast-feeding for the baby, and the sense of achievement for the mother. Then he moves on to a two-sided aspect of breast-feeding, the older baby's impulse to bite the nipple occasionally, which the baby himself learns to inhibit and which the mother also can inhibit, without vindictiveness, just by protecting herself. In a sense the baby has thus learned a new dimension of love, through aggressiveness; he has learned that a valued object such as the breast can survive his hostile impulses. These are the kinds of insights, gained from the psychoanalysis of adults and children, that show us the complexities of emotional development.

In "The Contribution of Psychoanalysis to Midwifery" Winnicott calls attention to the many disturbances in women's genital functioning, in menstruation and childbearing, that are at least partially due to emotional factors, and he congratulates midwives on being increasingly aware of these factors. He points out that a woman in labor cannot turn control of herself over to a professional unless she has come to know and trust her during the perinatal period.

The patient in labor and afterwards is highly sensitive to a too-dominating attitude on the part of midwife, nurse or baby nurse, often a carryover from a critical mother. With this in mind he begs the professionals not to try to take over the management of breast-feeding but leave it to the intuitive knowledge of the mother.

In a lecture called "Communication Between Infant and Mother, and Mother and Infant, Compared and Contrasted" Winnicott starts with the newborn baby's absolute dependence and matches this with the new mother's extraordinary, total preoccupation with him. It is so intense that it sometimes frightens a mother into thinking she has turned into a vegetable, but it only lasts a few weeks. It enables her to make a deep and crucial identification with her baby at the start. But she has also been prepared for this stage by having been a baby, played at being a baby and a mother, and regressed to babyhood during illness. For the baby it is all new; he recognizes no words, no time. He is ready to become human but must depend on an "ordinary devoted mother" to achieve it. She communicates by the inflections in her voice (the words don't matter), by her holding and handling and rocking. She communicates even by her breathing and her heartbeat, by meeting her baby's daily and gradually changing needs.

All this adds up to reliability and to love. But as Winnicott points out, even the best of human beings fail and fail often. In a sense this is how the infant comes to recognize the existence of reliability — by its occasional lapses. At the same time, mothers keep promptly mending their failures, and this, to mother and baby, adds up to adaptation and success. (Failures that are not mended constitute serious deprivations and bring developmental distortions.) Mother and baby also communicate on the common ground of playfulness and, most effectively, by the expressions on the mother's face, by the intuitive way the mother brings to the baby just what the baby is wanting — a change of position, a breast, a bottle — from which the baby acquires a sense of control, a sense of omnipotence and creativity.

As for the newborn baby's communication with the mother, Winnicott singles out the power of the baby's appearance of helplessness which renders the parent helpless to resist.

Finally I want to single out, as one source of *my* pleasure in reading Winnicott, the surprising contrasts in his language. It is predominately grave, deeply thoughtful and analytical. Then suddenly he gives way to earthy folk talk: "There is more to the baby than blood and bones." "She feels like shoving the breast into the baby's mouth or shoving the baby's mouth into the breast." "Then one day they [mothers] find they have become hostess to a new human being who has decided to take up lodging." "Damn you, you little bugger."

EDITORS' PREFACE

IN the years following Donald Winnicott's death in 1971 it was decided that the papers that he had left unpublished, together with those that had appeared only in journals and anthologies, should be published in collections under his own name.

The papers brought together in this book were written specifically about the psychological processes that take place in the infant around the time of birth and shortly thereafter, when "the baby and the mother are not yet separated out in the baby's rudimentary mind"; and they examine the implications that ensue for those who have care of newborn babies and their mothers.

We hope in particular that professional workers in this field will find the book valuable and enjoyable, and that it will reach a new generation of readers who can make use of Winnicott's ability to see the everlasting in the ephemeral.

London, 1986   RAY SHEPHERD
                                             MADELEINE DAVIS

BABIES AND THEIR MOTHERS

CHAPTER ONE

※

The Ordinary Devoted Mother

HOW to say something new on a well-worn subject? My name has become linked with these words, and first perhaps I should explain this.

I was walking, in the summer of 1949, to have drinks with the B.B.C. producer, Miss Isa Benzie, who now has retired and whose name I like to remember, and she was telling me that I could give a series of nine talks on any subject that might please me. She was, of course, on the lookout for a catchphrase, but I did not know this. I told her that I had no interest whatever in trying to tell people what to do. To start with, I didn't know. But I would like to talk to mothers about the thing that they do well, and that they do well simply because each mother is devoted to the task in hand, namely the care of one infant, or perhaps twins. I said that ordinarily this just happens, and it is the exception when a

NOTE: Information about sources, previous publication, or the original audience for each chapter can be found on p. 105. Eds.

baby has to do without being cared for at the start by a specialist. Isa Benzie picked up the clue in a matter of twenty yards, and she said: "Splendid! The Ordinary Devoted Mother." So that was that.

You can imagine that I have been ragged somewhat on account of this phrase, and there are many who assume that I am sentimental about mothers and that I idealise them, and that I leave out fathers, and that I can't see that some mothers are pretty awful if not in fact impossible. I have to put up with these small inconveniences because I am not ashamed of what is implied by these words.

There is another criticism that comes from those who have also heard me say that failure of mothers at the Ordinary Devoted Mother level is one factor in the aetiology of autism. It is felt to be an accusation when one really goes on logically and refers to the effects of Ordinary Devoted Mother failure. But is it not natural that if this thing called devotion is really important, then its absence or a relative failure in this area should have consequences that are untoward? I shall return to this theme when I come to discuss what is meant by the word *blame*.

I see that I cannot avoid saying the obvious. It is a trite remark when I say that by devoted I simply mean devoted. You have the job of doing the altar flowers for your church at the end of every week. If you take it on you simply do not forget. On Fridays you find yourself making sure the flowers are there to be arranged; or if you have the flu you begin telephoning round, or sending a message to someone by the milkman, even though you don't like to see them done well by someone else. It just doesn't happen that the congregation congregates on Sunday and the altar is bare or there are dead flowers in dirty vases disgracing instead of gracing the sanctuary. Yet, at the same time, it cannot be said, I hope, that you spend Monday to Thursday getting all worked up or worrying. The matter is simply lying asleep in the back of your mind, and it wakes up and wakes you up on Friday, or perhaps Saturday.

In a similar way women are not all the time fussing around thinking they ought to be looking after a baby. They play golf, they have a job that they lose themselves in, they quite naturally do all sorts of male things like being irresponsible, or taking everything for granted, or motor-racing. This is Monday to Friday, in terms of the altar flowers.

Then, one day, they find they have become hostess to a new human being who has decided to take up lodgings, and like the character played by Robert Morley in *The Man Who Came to Dinner*, to exercise a crescendo of demands till some date in the far-extended future when there will once again be peace and quiet; and they, these women, may return to self-expression of a more direct kind. During this prolonged Friday–Saturday–Sunday, they have been in a phase of self-expression through identification with what with luck grows into a baby, and becomes autonomous, biting the hand that fed it.

There happens to be this useful nine-months period in which there is time for a gradual change-over in the woman from the one kind of selfishness to the other. The same thing can be observed in fathers; also it is like this with people who decide to adopt a baby, who come round to the idea of adopting, and who get worked up, and who reach a point at which the baby must materialise — unfortunately for adopters there is sometimes a disappointment here, and by the time the baby is found they have gone over into not being so sure that they want one.

I want to stress the importance of this period of preparation. When I was a medical student, I had a friend who was a poet. He was one of several of us who shared some very good digs in the slums of North Kensington. This is how we found the digs:

My friend the poet, who was very tall and indolent and always smoking, walked down a terrace till he saw a house that looked friendly. He rang the bell. A woman came to the door and he liked the look of her face. So he said: "I want lodgings here." She said: "I have a vacancy. When will you be coming?" He said: "I have come." So he went in, and when he was shown the bedroom he said: "It happens that I am ill, so I will go straight to bed. What time can I have tea?" And he went to bed and stayed in bed for six months. In the course of a few days we had all settled in nicely, but the poet remained the landlady's favourite.

But nature has decreed that babies do not choose their mothers. They just turn up, and the mothers have time to re-orientate, to find that for a few months their orient is not in the east but is in the centre (or is it a bit off-centre?).

I suggest, as you know I do, and I suppose everyone agrees, that *ordinarily* the woman enters into a phase, a phase from which she *ordinarily* recovers in the weeks and months after the baby's birth, in which to a large extent she is the baby and the baby is her. There is nothing mystical about this. After all, she was a baby once, and she has in her the memories of being a baby; she also has memories of being cared for, and these memories either help or hinder her in her own experiences as a mother.

I think that by the time the baby is ripe for birth the mother, if properly cared for herself by her man or by the Welfare State or both, is ready for an experience in which she knows extremely well what are the baby's needs. You will understand I am not simply referring to her being able to know whether the baby is or is not hungry, and all that sort of thing; I am referring to innumerable subtle things, things that only my friend the poet could properly put into words. For my part, I am contented to use the world *hold*, and to extend its meaning to cover all that a mother is and does at this time. I believe it is a critical time, but I scarcely dare say this because it would be a pity to make a woman feel self-conscious just here where she is and where she acts naturally *naturally*. It is here that she cannot learn from books. She cannot use even Spock just at this point where she feels that the baby needs to be picked up, or put down, to be left alone or to be turned over, or where she knows that what is essential is the simplest of all experiences, that based on contact without activity, where there is opportunity for the feeling of oneness between two persons who are in fact two and not one. These things give the baby the opportunity to be, out of which there can arise the next things that have to do with action, doing and being done to. Here is the basis for what gradually becomes, for the infant, the self-experiencing being.

All this is highly tenuous, but repeated and repeated adds up to the foundation of the capacity in the baby to feel real. With this capacity the baby can face the world, or (I should say) can go ahead with the maturational processes which he or she inherits.

When these conditions obtain, as they usually do, the baby becomes able to develop the capacity to have feelings that correspond to some extent with those of the mother who is identified with her baby; or shall I say, heavily invested in her baby and in his or her care. At three or four months after being born the baby may be able to show that he or she knows what it is like to be a mother, that is a mother in her state of being devoted to something that is not in fact herself.

It must be remembered that what first appears at an early

age needs a long period of time to become established as a more or less fixed mechanism in the child's mental processes. What can be shown to have been present can indeed be lost, as is to be expected. But what I am concerned with here is that the more complex cannot arise except out of the most simple, and in health the complexity of the mind and personality develops gradually and by steady growth, always from simple to complex.

In time the baby begins to need the mother to fail to adapt — this failure being also a graduated process that cannot be learned from books. It would be irksome for a human child to go on experiencing omnipotence when the apparatus has arrived which can cope with frustrations and relative environmental failures. There is much satisfaction to be got from anger that does not go over into despair.

Any parent here will know what I mean when I say that although you subjected your baby to the most awful frustrations you never once let him (or her) down — that is, your ego support to the baby's ego was reliable. The baby never woke and cried and there was no one to hear. In later language you found you did not try to put your child off with lies.

But, of course, all this implies not only that the mother was able to give herself over to this preoccupation with the care of her infant, but also that she was lucky. I need not start to enumerate the things that may happen even in the best-regulated families. I will give three examples, however, to illustrate three types of trouble. The first is pure chance — a mother gets ill and dies, and she has to let her baby down exactly in the way that she hates to do. Or she starts up a new pregnancy before the time that she had thought out as appropriate. She might be to some extent responsible for this complication, but these things are not as simple as winking. Or a mother becomes depressed and she can feel herself depriving her child of what the child needs, but she cannot help the onset of a mood swing, which may quite easily be reactive to something that has impinged in her private life. Here she is causing trouble, but no one would blame her.

In other words there are all manner of reasons why some children do get let down before they are able to avoid being wounded or maimed in personality by the fact.

Here I must go back to the idea of blame. It is necessary for us to be able to look at human growth and development, with all its complexities that are internal or personal to the child, and we must be able to say: here the ordinary devoted mother factor failed, without blaming anyone. For my part I have no interest whatever in apportioning blame. Mothers and fathers blame themselves, but that is another matter, and indeed they blame themselves for almost anything, for having a mongol child, for instance, which they certainly could not be held responsible for.

But we must be able to look at aetiology and be able if necessary to say that some of the failures of development that we meet sprang from a failure of the ordinary devoted mother factor at a certain point or over a phase. This has nothing to do with moral responsibility. It is another subject. In any case, what good would I have been as a mother?

But I have one special reason why I feel we must be able to apportion aetiological significance (not blame), and that is that in no other way can we recognise the positive value of the ordinary devoted mother factor — the vital necessity for every baby that someone should facilitate the earliest stages of the processes of psychological growth, or psychosomatic growth, or shall I say the growth of the most immature and absolutely dependent human personality.

In other words, I do not believe in the story of Romulus

and Remus, much as I respect wolf bitches. Someone who was human found and cared for the founders of Rome, if indeed we are to allow any truth at all to this myth. I do not go on further and say we as men and women *owe* anything to the women who did this for each one of us severally. We owe nothing. But to ourselves we owe an intellectual recognition of the fact that at first we were (psychologically) absolutely dependent, and that absolutely means absolutely. Luckily we were met by ordinary devotion.

* * *

Is it possible to say something about the reasons why it is necessary that a mother should be able to make this very close adaptation to her child's needs at the beginning?[1] It is easy to say quite a lot about the more obvious although more complicated needs of older children and of children making the grade from being related simply to mother to triangular relationships. It is easy to see that children need a firm setting in which to work out their conflicts of love and hate and their two main trends, one based on an orientation to the parent of the same sex and the other based on an orientation to the parent of the other sex. This can be referred to as the hetero- and homosexual strivings in object-relating.

You will want me, however, to try to make a statement about the infant's needs in this very early stage where there nearly always is a mother-figure who is in the position of having nothing much else on her mind over a phase in which the baby's dependence is absolute. Elsewhere I have written quite a lot on this subject, and I cannot hope to do more than sum up if I am to refer to it in a few words. I want to say

---

[1] The following passages were found with the foregoing talk in Dr. Winnicott's papers. Eds.

that in these early, most significant weeks of the baby's life the initial stages of the maturational processes have their first opportunity to become experiences of the baby. Where there is good enough quality in the facilitating environment, which has to be a human one and a personal one, the inherited tendencies of the baby to grow have their first important achievements. One can give names to these things. The main thing is covered by the word *integration*. All the bits and pieces of activity and sensation which go to form what we come to know as this particular baby begin to come together at times so that there are moments of integration in which the baby is a unit although of course a highly dependent one. We say that the mother's ego support facilitates the ego organization of the baby. Eventually the baby becomes able to assert his or her own individuality and even to feel a sense of identity. The whole thing looks very simple when it goes well, and the basis for all this is in the very early relationship in which the baby and the mother are at one. There is nothing mystical about this. The mother has one kind of identification with the baby, a highly sophisticated one, in that she feels very much identified with the baby, but of course she remains adult. The baby, on the other hand, has an identity with the mother in the quiet moments of contact which is not so much an achievement of the baby as of the relationship which the mother makes possible. From the baby's point of view there is nothing else but the baby, and therefore the mother is at first part of the baby. In other words, there is something here which people call primary identification. There is the beginning of everything, and it gives meaning to very simple words like *being*.

We could use a Frenchified word *existing* and talk about existence, and we can make this into a philosophy and call it existentialism, but somehow or other we like to start with the word *being* and then with the statement *I am*. The important thing is that *I am* means nothing unless *I* at the beginning *am along with another human being* who has not yet been differentiated off. For this reason it is more true to talk about *being* than to use the words *I am*, which belong to the next stage. It cannot be overemphasized that being is the beginning of everything, without which *doing* and *being done to* have no significance. It is possible to seduce a baby into feeding and into the functioning of all the bodily processes, but the baby does not feel these things as an experience unless it is built on a quantity of simple being which is enough to establish the self that is eventually a person.

The opposite of integration is a failure of integration or disintegration from a state of integration. This is unbearable. It is one of the most basic unthinkable anxieties of infancy which are prevented by ordinary care of the kind that nearly all infants do, in fact, get from an adult human being. I will enumerate very briefly one or two other similar basic growth processes. It is not possible to take for granted that the infant's psyche will form satisfactorily in partnership with the soma, that is to say with the body and its functioning. Psycho-somatic existence is an achievement, and although its basis is an inherited growth tendency, it cannot become a fact without the active participation of a human being who is holding and handling the baby. A breakdown in this area has to do with all the difficulties affecting bodily health which actually stem from uncertainty in personality structure. You will see that the breakdown of these very early growth processes takes us immediately to the kind of symptomatology which we find in our mental hospitals so that the prevention of mental hospital disorder belongs initially to infant care and the things that come naturally to mothers who like having a baby to look after.

Another thing that I could mention has to do with the beginnings of object-relating. This is already getting on towards a sophisticated view of psychology. You will recognise, however, the way in which, when the relationship between the baby and the mother is satisfactory, objects begin to turn up which the baby can use symbolically; not only the thumb for sucking but also something to catch hold of which eventually may become a doll or a toy. A breakdown here has to be measured in terms of a failure of the capacity for object-relating.

It will be observed that though at first we were talking about very simple things, we were also talking about matters that have vital importance, matters that concern the laying down of the foundations for mental health. A great deal of course is done at later stages, but it is when the beginning is good that all that is done at later stages can take effect. Sometimes mothers find it alarming to think that what they are doing is so important and in that case it is better not to tell them. It makes them self-conscious and then they do everything less well. It is not possible to learn these matters, and anxiety is no substitute for this very simple kind of love which is almost physical. It might be asked, why then bother to point all this out? But I do want to emphasize that someone must bother about these things because otherwise we forget the importance of the very early relationships and we interfere too easily. This is something we must absolutely never do. When a mother has a capacity quite simply to be a mother we must never interfere. She will not be able to fight for her rights because she will not understand. All she will know is that she has been wounded. Only the wound is not a broken bone or a gash in her arm. It is the maimed personality of the baby. How often a mother spends years of her life trying to mend this wound which in fact was caused by us when we unnecessarily interfered with something that was so simple that it seemed to be unimportant.

[1966]

CHAPTER TWO

Knowing and Learning

THERE is much for a young mother to learn. She gets told useful things by experts, about the introduction of solids into the diet, about vitamins, and about the use of the weight chart: and then sometimes she gets told about quite a different kind of thing, for instance, about her reaction to her infant's refusal of food.

It seems to me to be important for you[1] to be quite clear about the difference between these two types of knowledge. What you do and know, simply by virtue of the fact that you are the mother of an infant, is as far apart from what you know by learning as is the east from the west coast of England. I cannot put this too strongly. Just as the professor who found out about the vitamins that prevent rickets really has something to teach you, so you really have something to teach him about the other kind of knowledge, that which comes to you naturally.

[1]Winnicott was addressing mothers here. See p. 105. Eds.

The mother who breast-feeds her baby simply does not have to bother about fats and proteins while she is thoroughly caught up in the management of the early stages. By the time she weans at nine months or so and the baby is making fewer demands on her, she is becoming free to study facts and advice which doctors and nurses offer. Obviously there is a great deal that she could not know intuitively, and she does want to be told about the giving of solids, and about how to use the sort of foods that are available in such a way that the baby will be able to grow and keep healthy. But she must wait for such instruction until she is in a state of mind to receive it.

We can easily see that years of brilliant research have gone into the doctor's bit of advice about vitamins, and we can look with awe at the scientist's work and at the self-discipline that such work entails, and be grateful when, by the results of scientific research, a great deal of suffering can be avoided, perhaps by some quite simple advice like adding a few drops of cod-liver oil to the diet.

At the same time the scientist, if he cares to do so, may look with awe at the mother's intuitive understanding, which makes her able to care for her infant without learning. In fact, the essential richness of this intuitive understanding, I would say, is that it *is* natural and unspoiled by learning.

The difficult task, in preparing a series of talks and books on infant care, is to know how to avoid disturbance of what comes naturally to mothers while getting them informed accurately as to the useful facts that emerge from scientific research.

I want you to be able to feel confident about your capacity as mothers, and not feel that because you could not know about vitamins, you also could not know about, for instance, how to hold your infant.

How to hold your infant; that would be a good example for me to follow up.

The phrase "holding the baby" has a definite meaning in the English language; someone was co-operating with you over something, and then waltzed off, and you were left "holding the baby." By this we can see that everybody knows that mothers naturally have a sense of responsibility, and if they have a baby in their arms they are involved in some special way. Of course, some women get left holding the baby literally, in the sense that the father is unable to enjoy the part he has to play, and unable to share with the mother the great responsibility which a baby must always be to someone.

Or perhaps there is no father. Ordinarily, however, the mother feels supported by her husband and so is free to be a mother properly, and when she holds her baby she does it naturally, and without thinking it out. Such a mother will be surprised if I talk about such a thing as holding a baby as a skilled job.

When people see a baby they love to be able to be allowed to experience just this thing, of holding the baby in their arms. You don't let people hold your baby if you feel it means nothing to them. Babies are very sensitive indeed to the way they are held, so that they cry with one person and rest contented with another, even when they are quite tiny. Sometimes a little girl will ask to hold a newly-arrived baby brother or sister, and this is a big event. The wise mother will remember not to give the child the whole responsibility, and will be there all the time if she lets this happen, ready to take the baby back into her own safe keeping. The wise mother will certainly not just take it for granted that an older sister is safe with the baby in her arms. This would be to deny the meaning of it all. I know people who can remember throughout their lives the awful feeling of holding the baby brother or sister, and of the nightmare of not feeling safe. In the nightmare the baby is dropped. The fear which can turn up in the nightmare as doing harm in practice makes the big sister catch hold of the baby too tightly.

All this leads on to what you do yourself quite naturally because of your devotion to your baby. You are not anxious and so are not gripping too tight. You are not afraid you will throw the baby on to the floor. You just adapt the pressure of your arms to the baby's needs, and you move slightly, and you perhaps make some sounds. The baby feels you breathing. There is warmth that comes from your breath and your skin, and the baby finds your holding to be good.

Of course there are all kinds of mothers, and there are some who are not quite so happy about the way they hold their babies. Some feel a bit doubtful; the baby seems happier in the cot. There may be something left over in such a mother of the fear which she had to deal with when she was a little girl, when her mother let her hold a newborn baby. Or she may have had a mother who was not very good at this sort of thing herself, and she is afraid of passing on to her baby some uncertainty belonging to the past. An anxious mother uses the cot as much as possible, or even hands the baby over to the care of a nurse, carefully chosen because of the natural way she handles babies. There is room for all kinds of mothers in the world, and some will be good at one thing and some good at another. Or shall I say some will be bad at one thing and some bad at another? Some are anxious holders.

It may be worth while looking even a little more closely at this business, because if you do handle your baby well I want you to be able to know that you are doing something of importance. This is a little part of the way in which you give a good foundation for the mental health of this new member of the community.

Look at it imaginatively.

Here is the infant right at the beginning (from what happens at the beginning we can see what happens, over and over again, later on). Let me describe three stages in the infant's relation to the world (represented by your arms and your breathing body), leaving out hunger and anger, and all the great upheavals. First stage: the infant is self-contained, a live creature, yet surrounded by space. The infant knows of nothing, except of self. Second stage: the infant moves an elbow, a knee, or straightens out a little. The space has been crossed. The infant has surprised the environment. Third stage: you who are holding the infant jump a little, because the door bell rang, or the kettle boiled over, and again the space has been crossed. This time the environment has surprised the infant.

First, the self-contained infant is in the space that is maintained between the child and the world, then the infant surprises the world, and thirdly, the world surprises the infant. This is so simple that I think it will appeal to you as a natural sequence, and therefore a good basis for the study of the way you hold your infant.

This is all very obvious, but the trouble is that if you do not know these things you may easily let your immense skill get wasted, because you will not see how to explain to neighbours, and to your husband, how necessary it is for you, in your turn, to have a space to yourself in which you can start your infant off with a sound basis for life.

Let me put it this way. The baby in the space becomes ready, in the course of time, for the movement that surprises the world, and the infant who has found the world in this way becomes, in time, ready to welcome the surprises that the world has in store.

The baby does not know that the space around is maintained by you. How careful you are that the world shall not impinge before the infant has found it! By a live and breathing quietness you follow the life in the infant with the life in yourself, and you wait for the gestures that come from the infant, gestures that lead to your being discovered.

If you feel heavy with sleep, and especially if you are in a depressed mood, you put the infant in a cot, because you know that your sleeping state is not alive enough to keep going the infant's idea of a space around.

If I have referred specially to tiny infants, and your management of them, this does not mean that I am not also referring to older children. Of course most of the time the older child has passed through to a much more complex state of affairs, and is not in need of the very special management which comes naturally to you when you are holding your baby who is only a few hours old. But how often it happens that the older child, just for a few minutes, or for an hour or two, needs to go back, and to go over the ground again that belongs to the earliest stages. Perhaps your child has had an accident, and comes to you crying. It may be five or ten minutes before there is a return to play. In the meantime you have had the child in your arms, and you have allowed for just this same sequence that I have been talking about. First of all, the quiet yet live holding, and then the readiness for the child to move and to find you, as the tears clear away. And at length you are able, quite naturally, to put the child down. Or a child is unwell, or sad, or tired. Whatever it is, for a little while the child is an infant, and you know that time has to be given so that there can be a natural return from essential security to ordinary conditions.

Of course I might have chosen many other examples of the way in which you have knowledge, simply because you are specialists in this particular matter of the care of your own children. I want to encourage you to keep and defend this specialist knowledge. It cannot be taught. Then you can learn things from other kinds of specialist. Only if you can keep what is natural in you is it safe for you to learn anything that doctors and nurses can teach you.

It might be thought that I have been trying to teach you now how to hold your baby. This seems to me to be far from the truth. I am trying to describe various aspects of the things you do naturally, in order that you may be able to recognise what you do, and in order that you may be able to get the feeling of your natural capacity. This is important, because unthinking people will often try to teach you how to do the things which you can *do* better than you can be *taught* to do them. If you are sure of all this, you can start to add to your value as a mother by learning the things that can be taught, for the best of our civilisation and culture offers much that is of value, if you can take it without the loss of what comes to you naturally.

[1950]

CHAPTER THREE

Breast-feeding
as Communication

I COME to this subject as a paediatrician turned psychoanalyst and as one with a long experience of the sort of case that turns up in the practice of a child psychiatrist. In order to do my work I have to have a theory of the *emotional* as well as the *physical* development of the individual child in the environment that obtains, and a theory needs to cover the whole range of what may be expected. At the same time theory needs to be flexible so that any clinical fact may if necessary modify the theoretical statement.

I am not specifically concerned with promoting and encouraging breast-feeding, although I do hope that the general trend of what I have had to say in the course of years about this matter has had exactly this effect, simply because here is something natural and it is likely that what is natural has a very good foundation.

What I want to do first is to dissociate myself from a sentimental attitude towards breast-feeding or propaganda in favour of breast-feeding. Propaganda always has another side to it which eventually turns up as a reaction to the propaganda. There is no doubt whatever that a vast number of individuals in this world today have been brought up satisfactorily without having had the experience of breast-feeding. This means that there are other ways by which an infant may experience physical intimacy with the mother. Nevertheless I myself would always be sorry if breast-feeding fails in any one case, simply because I believe that the mother or the baby or both are losing something if they lose this experience.

We are not just simply concerned with illness or with psychiatric disturbances; we are concerned with the richness of the personality and strength of character and with the capacity for happiness, as well as the capacity for revolution and revolt. It is likely that true strength belongs to the individual's experience of the developmental process along *natural* lines, and this is what we hope for in individuals. In practice this kind of strength becomes easily lost sight of because of the comparable strength that can come from fear and resentment and deprivation and the state of never having had.

If attention is given to the teachings of the paediatricians one may wonder whether breast-feeding is better than other kinds of feeding. Some paediatricians actually believe that artificial feeding if done well can be more satisfactory in terms of anatomy and physiology, which are their concerns. We need not feel that the subject is ended when the paediatrician has finished talking, especially if he seems to forget that there is more about a baby than blood and bones. From my point of view the mental health of the individual is being laid down from the very beginning by the mother who provides what I have called a facilitating environment, that is to say one in which the infant's natural growth processes and interactions with the environment can evolve according to the inherited pattern of the individual. The mother is (without knowing it) laying down the foundations of mental health of the individual.

But not only that. If we assume mental health, the mother (if she is doing well) is laying down the foundations of the individual's strength of character and richness of personality. On such a good basis the individual has a chance as time goes on to reach to the world creatively and to enjoy and use what the world has to offer, including the cultural heritage. It is unfortunately only too true that if a child is not started off well enough then the cultural heritage might just as well never have been and the beauty of the world is only a tantalising colour that cannot be enjoyed. In this way therefore there are truly the haves and the have-nots, and this has nothing to do with finance; it has to do with those who were started off well enough and those who were not started off well enough.

The matter of breast-feeding is certainly part and parcel of this vast problem, part of what we mean when we say that someone is started off by being given a good enough environmental provision. It is not the whole story, however. Psychoanalysts who are responsible for the theory of the emotional development of the individual which we use in this modern age have been responsible to some extent for putting forward the actual breast in a somewhat over-emphasized way. They were not wrong. In the course of time, however, we have come to see that a "good breast" is a jargon word, and it means satisfactory mothering and parentage in a general way. For instance, holding and handling are more vitally important as indications of management than is the actual fact of a breast-feeding experience. Also it is well known that many babies have what seems to be a satisfactory breast-feeding experience and yet they are unsatisfactory in the sense that there is already an observable defect in their developmental process and in their capacity to relate to people and to make use of objects — a defect due to poor holding and handling.

Once I have made it quite clear that the word *breast* and the idea of breast-feeding is an expression that carries with it the whole technique of being a mother to a baby then I am free to point out how important *the breast itself* can be, and I will try to do this. You will perhaps see what I am trying to get away from. I want to dissociate myself from those who try to *make* mothers breast-feed their babies. I have seen a great number of children who were given a very bad time with a mother struggling to make the breast work, which of course she is completely unable to do because it is outside conscious control. The mother suffers and the baby suffers. Sometimes great relief is experienced when at last bottle-feeding is established and at any rate something is going well in the sense that the baby is getting satisfied by taking in the right quantity of suitable food. Many of these struggles could be avoided if the religion were taken out of this idea of breast-feeding. It seems to me the ultimate insult, to a woman who would *like* to breast-feed her child and who comes naturally to doing so, if some authority, a doctor or a nurse, comes along and says "You *must* breast-feed your baby." If I were a woman this would be enough to put me off. I would say: "Very well then I won't." Unfortunately mothers have this terrible belief in doctors and nurses, and they think that because the doctor knows what to do if things go wrong, or should an acute surgical emergency arise, therefore the doctor knows how to get a mother and baby into relationship with each other. Usually he has no understanding whatever of this which is a matter of intimacy between mother and baby.

It is a question of getting doctors and nurses in general to understand that while they are needed, and very much needed, in case things go wrong on the physical side, they are not specialists in the matters of intimacy that are vital to both the mother and the baby. If they start to give advice about intimacy, they are on dangerous ground because neither the mother nor the baby needs advice. Instead of advice what they need is an environmental provision which fosters the mother's belief in herself. It is a very important modern development that is more and more common for the father to be able to be present when a baby is being born, and the father can bring to the situation an understanding of the importance of the first moments when the mother can take a look at her baby before taking a rest. It is the same with the establishment of breast-feeding. It is something which can become very difficult because the mother is unable to feed by the breast by deliberate effort. She has to wait for her own reactions, or on the other hand her reactions are so strong that she can hardly wait for the baby and has to be helped because of the dammed-up milk.

In regard to educating doctors and nurses in this matter, however, it must be remembered that they have so much else to learn because the demands of modern medicine and surgery are very great indeed. And doctors and nurses are quite ordinary people. It is for parents to know and to be self-conscious about their own needs at this very early stage and to insist on self-fulfillment. Just occasionally it is possible for parents to find doctors and nurses who understand what is their own function and what is the function of the parents, and then the partnership is always a very happy one. Naturally from my position I hear a very great deal from mothers about the distress caused by doctors and nurses who, while being first-rate on the physical side, cannot avoid interfering and being the opposite of helpful in the matter of the inter-relationship of mother and father and baby.

There are of course mothers who have very big personal difficulties belonging to their own inner conflicts and perhaps related to their own experiences as infants. These matters can sometimes be sorted out. Where a mother has a difficulty about breast-feeding it is wrong to try to force a situation which must to some extent fail and may become a disaster. It is therefore very bad practice for those in charge to have a preconceived notion about what a mother ought to do in regard to breast-feeding. It often happens that a mother must give up early and institute another kind of feeding, and she may succeed with her second or third child and be very glad that this came to her in a natural way. Where a baby is not to be fed at the breast there are many other ways in which the mother can allow intimacy of a physical kind.

I would like to illustrate at this point the way in which these matters may be of importance at a very early stage. Here is a woman who adopted a baby at six weeks. What she found was that the baby responded well to human contact and to cuddling and to the usual holding and handling aspects of baby care. Already at six weeks, however, the mother discovered that the baby had a pattern derived from previous experience. This pattern was related only to the feeding situation. To get the baby to feed she had to put her on the floor or on a hard table, and without physical contact of any other kind hold the bottle so that the baby could respond by sucking. This abnormal feeding pattern persisted and wove itself into the texture of the child's personality and showed quite clearly to anyone watching the child's development that the very early experience of impersonal feeding had had an effect, and in this case not a good effect.

If I were to continue to give illustrative material I would only confuse the issue because the subject covers a wide range, and it is better for me to call on the experiences of those who are listening to me and to remind you that the little tiny things that happen between the mother and baby at the beginning are significant and not less so because they seem so natural and seem to be best taken for granted.

I come therefore to the positive value of breast-feeding working on the basis that breast-feeding is not absolutely essential and should not be persisted in where the mother has a personal difficulty. The obvious part of what I wish to say has to do with the tremendous richness that belongs to the feeding experience; the baby is awake and alive and the whole of the emerging personality is engaged. A great deal of the baby's waking life at first has to do with feeding. In a way, the baby is gathering stuff for dreaming, although soon there are all the other things that also become gathered in and which can reverberate in the inner reality of the sleeping child, who is of course dreaming. Doctors are so used to talking about health and disease that sometimes they forget to talk about the tremendous variations in health, variations which make it true that whereas one child's experience is weak, colourless, and even boring, another child's experience is almost too exciting, too full of colour and sensation and qualitative richness to be bearable. For some babies feeding experiences are so boring that it must be quite a relief to cry with anger and frustration, which at any rate can feel real and must involve the total personality. The first thing to do, therefore, in looking at a baby's breast-feeding experience is to think in terms of the *richness* of the experience and the involvement of the total personality. Many of the important features of the breast-feeding situation can be seen to be there when the bottle is used. For instance, the baby and the mother looking into each other's eyes, which is a feature at the early stage, does not absolutely depend on the use of the actual breast. Nevertheless one is left with a guess that on the whole the taste and smell and sensuous experience of a breast-feeding is something that is absent when the baby engages with a rubber teat. No doubt babies have ways round even this disadvantage and in some cases the overestimation in the sensuous use of rubber can be traced back to the overestimation of rubber in the bottle-feeding experience. The baby's capacity for sensuous experience can be seen in the use of what I have called transitional objects where there is all the difference in the world for the baby between silk, nylon, wool, cotton, linen, a starched apron, rubber, and a wet napkin. This is another subject, however, to which I am making reference only to remind you of the fact that in the little world of the baby tremendous things happen.

Alongside the observation of the baby's experiences which are richer when the breast is being used than with a bottle, one has to put all that the mother herself feels and experiences. I need hardly start on this big subject, attempting to describe the sense of achievement which the mother may feel when physiology and anatomy which have been rather a nuisance to her perhaps suddenly make sense and she is able to deal with the fear that the baby will eat her by finding that in fact she has something called milk with which to fob the baby off. I prefer to leave it to your imagination, but it is important to draw attention to the fact that although the feeding of a baby can be very satisfactory, however it is done, the satisfaction is of a different order altogether for the woman who is able to use a part of her own body in this way. The satisfaction links up with her own experiences when she was a baby, and the whole thing goes back to the beginning of time when human beings had scarcely moved from the position of mammalian animal life.

I now come to what I consider to be the most important observation in this field. This has to do with the fact that there is aggressiveness in the live baby. In the course of time the baby begins to kick and scream and scratch. In the feeding situation there was very powerful gum action at the beginning, action of a kind that can very easily cause cracked nipples; and some babies actually hang on with their gums and hurt quite a lot. One cannot say that they are trying to hurt, because there is not enough baby there yet for aggression to mean anything. In the course of time, however, babies have an impulse to bite. This is the beginning of something that has tremendous importance. It belongs to the whole area of ruthlessness and impulse and the use of unprotected objects. Very, very quickly babies protect the breast, and in fact even when babies have teeth they but seldom bite to do damage.

This is not because they do not have the impulse; it is because of something which corresponds to the domestication of the wolf into a dog, and a lion into a cat. With human babies, however, there is a very difficult stage which cannot be avoided. The mother can easily see the baby through this stage in which she is being sometimes destroyed by her baby if she can know about it and protect herself without becoming retaliatory and vindictive.

In other words she has one job when the baby bites and scratches and pulls her hair and kicks, and that is to survive. The baby will do the rest. If she survives, then the baby will find a new meaning to the word love, and a new thing turns up in the baby's life which is fantasy. It is as if the baby can now say to the mother: "I love you because you have survived my destruction of you. In my *dreams* and in *my fantasy*

I destroy you whenever I think of you because I love you."
It is this that objectifies the mother, puts her in a world that
is not part of the baby, and makes her useful.

You can see that we are talking about a baby who is over
six months old, and we are talking about a child of two years.
We are finding a language which is important in the general
description of the child's forward development in which he
becomes part of the world instead of living in a protected
specialised or subjective world produced by the mother's tremendous capacity to adapt to his needs. But do not let us
deny the rudiments of these later things even to the
newborn.

It is not our job here to go into this transition which is so
important in the life of every child and enables the child to
be a part of the world and to use the world and to contribute
to the world. The thing that is important here is the recognition of the fact that the basis for this healthy development
in the human individual is the survival of the object that has
been attacked. In the case of a mother feeding a baby it is
her survival not only as a live person, but also as a person
who did not change at the critical moment into a vindictive
person and did not retaliate. Quite soon other people, including the father, animals and toys, play the same part. It
can be seen how tricky it is for the mother to separate out
the weaning from the breast from this matter of the survival
of the object that has just come up for destruction because of
the baby's natural developmental processes. Without going
into the extremely interesting complications that belong to
this subject it is possible to say quite simply that the essential
feature is the survival of the object against this background.
It is now possible to look and see the difference between the
breast and the bottle. In all cases the survival of the mother
is central. Nevertheless, surely there is a difference between

the survival of a part of the mother's body and the survival of a bottle. As a comment on this one can cite the extremely traumatic experience for a baby of the breaking of a bottle during the feed as when, for instance, the nursing mother drops the bottle on the floor. Sometimes it is the baby who pushes the bottle over and breaks it.

Perhaps from this observation you can come to it at your own speed and see with me that the survival of a breast which is a part of the mother has a significance which is entirely of a different order from the significance of the survival of a glass bottle. These considerations make me look at breast-feeding as another of those natural phenomena that justify themselves, even if they can, when necessary, be bypassed.

[1968]

CHAPTER FOUR

The Newborn and His Mother

THIS subject is so complex that I hesitate to add a new dimension. Nevertheless, it seems to me that if psychology has validity in the study of the newborn, it is only practice that it complicates.[1] In the theoretical realm, any contribution must be either wrong (in which case it leaves the problem untouched), or else has an element of truth in it, in which case it simplifies in the way that truth always does simplify.

The newborn and the mother — the Nursing Couple — is rather a wide subject, and yet I would not like the task of describing what is known about the newborn solo. It is psychology that is under discussion, and I like to assume that if we see a baby, we also see environmental provision, and behind this, we see the mother.

If I say "the mother" more often than "the father," I hope fathers will understand.

[1]Winnicott was addressing paediatricians here. See p. 105. Eds.

It is necessary to recognise the extreme difference that there must be between the mother's psychology and that of the infant. The mother is a sophisticated person. The baby at the beginning is the opposite of sophisticated. Many do not find it easy to ascribe anything that could be called "psychological" to an infant until some weeks or even months have passed, and it must be said that it is doctors rather than mothers who have this difficulty. Could we not say that mothers must be expected to see more than is there, and scientists must be expected to see nothing unless it is first proved?

I heard it said that it is in the newborn that physiology and psychology are one (John Davis).[2] This is a good start. Psychology is a gradual extension from physiology. There is no need for quarrelling over the date of this change. It could be variable according to events. However, the birthdate could be taken as a time when big changes occur in this field, so that the premature infant may be far better off psychologically in an incubator, whereas a postmature infant would not thrive in one but would need human arms and body contact.

It is a special thesis of mine that mothers, unless they are psychiatrically ill, do orientate to their very specialised task during the last months of pregnancy, and that they gradually recover from this in the course of weeks and months after the birth process. I have written a lot about this under the heading: "primary maternal preoccupation." In this state mothers become able to put themselves into the infant's shoes, so to speak. That is to say, they develop an amazing capacity for identification with the baby, and this makes them able to meet the basic needs of the infant in a way that no machine

---

[2] Paediatric colleague of Winnicott at Paddington Green Children's Hospital. Eds.

can imitate, and no teaching can reach. May I take this for granted when I go on to state that the prototype of all infant care is holding? And I mean human holding. I am aware that I am stretching the meaning of the word "holding" to its limits, but I suggest that this is an economical statement, and true enough.

An infant who is held well enough is quite a different thing from one who has not been held well enough. No observation on any infant has any value for me if the quality of the holding is not expressly described. For instance we have just seen a film which had special value for me. A doctor was holding a baby who was walking, illustrating primary walking; if you watched the doctor's tongue you could see that he was being very careful and sensitive, and that the baby was not behaving in the same way that he would behave if somebody else were doing the holding. I think that paediatricians on the whole are people who are able to identify with the infant and to hold an infant, and perhaps it is this capacity to identify that draws people to paediatrics. It seems to me that it is worth mentioning this very obvious point here because sometimes great variations are described in the way an infant behaves, and I think always we should have a film of who it is that is doing the investigation, so that we can judge for ourselves whether this was someone who knew what the infant was feeling like at that time. The reason why this special property of infant care must be mentioned, even in this brief statement, is that in the early stages of emotional development, before the senses have been organised, before there is something there that could be called an autonomous ego, very severe anxieties are experienced. In fact, the word "anxiety" is of no use, the order of infant distress at this stage being of the same order as that which lies behind panic, and panic is already a defence against the agony that makes people commit suicide rather than remember. I have meant to use strong language here. You see two infants; one has been held (in my extended sense of the word) well enough, and there is nothing to prevent a rapid emotional growth, according to inborn tendencies. The other has not had the experience of being held well and growth has had to be distorted and delayed, and some degree of primitive agony has to be carried on into life and living. Let it be said that in the common experience of good-enough holding the mother has been able to supply an auxiliary ego-function, so that the infant has had an ego from an early start, a very feeble, personal ego, but one boosted by the sensitive adaptation of the mother and by her ability to identify with her infant in relation to basic needs. The infant who has not had this experience has either needed to develop premature ego functioning, or else there has developed a muddle.

I find that I must make a bare statement because it is not necessarily true that those who are experienced on the physical side will know anything much about psychological theory. In the psychology of emotional growth the individual's maturational processes, if they are to become actual, need the provision of a facilitating environment. This latter, the facilitating environment, rapidly becomes extremely complex. Only a human being can know an infant in a way that makes possible an increasing complexity of adaptation that is graded to the infant's changing needs. Maturation in the early stages, and indeed all along, is very much a matter of integration. I cannot repeat here all that has been written on details of primitive emotional development, but three main tasks come under this heading: integration of the self, the psyche dwelling in the body, and object-relating. Roughly corresponding to these are the three functions of the mother: holding, handling, and object-presenting. Here is an immense subject in itself. I have made an attempt to state this in "The First Year of Life"[3] but at the moment I am trying to keep nearer to the birthdate.

You will see that I am trying to draw attention to the fact that babies are human from the beginning, that is, assuming that they have a suitable electronic apparatus. I know that here it is not necessary for me to draw attention to the fact that babies are human. This is the common denominator of psychology which belongs to paediatrics.

It is difficult to find a way of stating the beginnings of persons. If someone is there (one could say) to collect experiences, to collate them, to feel and to distinguish between feelings, to be apprehensive at the appropriate moment and to begin to organise defences against mental pain, then I would say the infant IS, and the study of the infant from this point onwards needs to include psychology. [See Chapter 5.]

You will be familiar with various attempts that are being made to study infants by direct observation. Here I need do no more than refer to the bibliography at the end of the recent book: *Determinants of Infant Behavior, Vol. 2.*[4] I shall not be dealing specifically with this type of work, and it might be asked: Why not? since direct observation is needed to make sense to those (and there are many here) whose main line of country is physical science. But I would prefer in these few minutes to try to hand over to you a tiny little bit of my experience as a psychoanalyst and as a psychiatrist of children. I came to this a long time ago out of the practice of physical paediatrics.

How can psychoanalysis bring light to bear on the psychology of the newborn? Obviously a great deal could be

[3] In *The Family and Individual Development*. London: Tavistock Publications, 1965.
[4] Ciba Foundation. London: Tavistock Publications, 1961–. Eds.

said here about psychiatric quirks in the mother, or father; but to make matters manageable, I must assume some health in the parents and study the infant, and I shall also assume physical health in the infant.

Psychoanalysis came to the rescue in the first place by providing a theory of emotional development — the only theory, really. But infantile matters were only seen, in early psychoanalysis, in the symbolism of dreams, in the stuff of psychosomatic symptomatology, in imaginative play. Gradually, psychoanalysis was extended backwards in time to apply to even small children, say two and a half years. This did not give what is needed for our purpose here, however, since little children of two and a half years are a surprisingly long way away from their infancy, unless they are ill and immature.

I am suggesting that the most important development in psychoanalysis, from our point of view here, is the extension of the work of the analyst to include the study of psychotic patients. It is being found that whereas psychoneurosis takes the analyst to the patient's young childhood, schizophrenia takes the analyst to the patient's infancy, to the start, to a stage of almost absolute dependence. Briefly, failures of the facilitating environment have been experienced in these cases at a stage before the immature and dependent ego has acquired a capacity to organise defences.

To narrow down the field still further, the best patient for the research worker who studies the psychology of infancy in this way is the borderline schizophrenic, that is, one who has sufficient functioning personality to be able to come to analysis and to do the irksome work that is necessary if the very ill part of the personality is to gain relief. I can do very little more than introduce you to the way that a severely regressed patient in a steady-going analytic treatment can en-

rich our understanding of the infant. In effect, the infant is
there on the couch, or on the floor or somewhere, and the
dependence is there in full strength, the analyst's auxiliary
ego function is active, the observation of the infant can be
direct except that the patient is an adult who has of course a
degree of sophistication. We have to allow for this sophistication which distorts the lens.

I want it to be known that I am aware of the distortions,
and that nothing I say is intended to prove anything, though
it may illustrate. Here are two examples of my attempt to
show that I know something about the *distortions*. First, a
schizophrenic boy, aged four. His mother and father are
doing the nursing. He has been given very special attention,
and as it is not a very severe case he is gradually recovering.
In my room he is playing at being born again from his
mother. He puts her legs out straight while he is on her lap,
and he dives down her legs on to the floor; this is a thing he
goes on doing over and over again. It is a particular game
derived out of special relationship with the mother, which
belongs to the fact of her having become a mental nurse of
an ill child instead of a mother. Now this game involves symbolism; it joins up with all the things that ordinary, normal
people like doing; and it joins up with the way being born
appears in dreams. But is this a direct memory that this boy
has of being born? Actually it cannot be so because he was
born by caesarian section. The point I am trying to make is
that any attempt to see the past in a patient has to be cor-
rected the whole time, and I know this, yet the symbolism
holds good.

Second, here is an hysterical woman "remembering" her
birth. She goes on to remember it in great detail and she has
anxiety dreams about it, and actually in one of the dreams
there is the doctor coming, and he has a frock-coat and a top-

hat on, and he has a bag, and she remembers what he said to her mother. This, of course, is a typical hysterical distortion, although it does not rule out the possibility that this woman was *also* dealing with actual birth memories. This type of dream material cannot be used in this discussion, and of course she knew about birth processes as an adult, and she had a lot of siblings born after her.

By contrast, I can give a picture of a little child of two playing the part of her new baby sister that was being born. She was trying to get through to a new relationship to the little sister. There was a specific thing that we had to do. She came in and she knew what she wanted, and she put me on the floor amongst the toys and I had to be "herself." Then she went and she got her father in to the room from the waiting-room (mother would have done, but father was there), and she sat on his lap, and now she was going to be the baby being born. To do this she jumped around on father's lap and then she went zoop down to the floor through his legs and she said: "I'm a baby!" And then she watched me and I had a specific function. I was acting her part, you see, and she told me more or less what to do, and I had to be very angry and to knock over toys and say: "I don't want a baby sister" and all that sort of thing, and this had to go on over and over again. You see how easy it was for this little girl to play the birth process by diving down, and she did it about ten times, until her father couldn't stand it any longer, and then she started getting born out of the top of his head; of course, he did not mind that so much because he is a professor and very clever in the head.

I am going to try to get down to some work now, and I would like to talk about the Moro Response. In any case you are all familiar with it, and I do not need to describe how, when the head of the baby is dropped a little, the baby reacts in a predictable way. Here is a detail of what I call *not good enough mothering*, isolated for the purpose of scientific study. This is exactly what a mother would *not* do to her infant. I mean, the reason why doctors do not get slapped in the face when they do it to the infants is because they are doctors, and mothers are frightened of doctors. Of course, one Moro Response does not upset an infant's psychology, but if you were to consider that an infant happened to be born to a mother who just had a thing about the Moro Response and every twenty minutes or so she would just take her infant up and drop the infant's head to see what would happen, this infant would not have a good enough mother. So it is exactly what a mother would not do to her infant. While a mother may have no words to describe her feelings for her baby, when she lifts him, she gathers him together.

Now I want to go over to the analytic treatment of a woman patient. This woman needed a deep and prolonged regression to dependence. Her treatment has lasted many, many years. It has provided me with a unique opportunity for watching infancy, infancy appearing in an adult. The baby who is being tested for Moro Response cannot talk about what happened. On the other hand, the woman, when she recovers from each phase of deep regression, becomes an adult with knowledge and sophistication. She can talk. Allowance has to be made for the complication that she is not only an infant but also a sophisticated person.

In the very early stage of emotional development to which this woman regressed there is a very simple idea of the self. In fact, with good enough mothering, there need be only the very beginnings of an idea of the self, or should I say, none at all. The bad holding (or the environmental failure that elicited the Moro Response) forces on the infant a premature awareness for which the infant is ill-equipped. If the baby could talk, he or she would say: "Here I was, enjoying a continuity of being. I had no thought as to the appropriate diagram for my self, but it could have been a circle." (Interrupting the baby here, it seems to me that people who make the balloons sold in the park on Easter Monday, for instance — it's the same in England — forget that what children like is a simple sphere that doesn't obey the laws of gravity. They don't want ears and noses, and writing on it, and all sorts of things like that). "A diagram of my self could have been a circle." (This is the baby talking) "Suddenly two terrible things happened; the continuity of my going on being, which is all I have at present of personal integration, was interrupted, and it was interrupted by my having to be in two parts, a body and a head. The new diagram that I was suddenly forced to make of myself was one of two unconnected circles instead of the one circle that I didn't even have to know about before this awful thing happened." The baby is trying to describe a personality split and also premature awareness produced by the dropping of the head.

The fact is that the infant was subjected to mental pain, and it is just this mental pain that the schizophrenic carries round as a memory and a threat, and that makes suicide a sensible alternative to living.

I have not finished with my woman patient yet. You may ask why it is that there is a drive in my patient to regress to dependence, and I first must answer this. In the so-called "borderline" case there is a drive towards progress in the emotional development that has been held up. There is no way of remembering very early experiences except by a re-experiencing of them, and as these experiences were excessively painful at the time, because they came when the ego was unorganised and the auxiliary ego of the mothering was faulty, the re-experiencing has to be done in a carefully prepared and tested situation, such as the setting provided by the psychoanalyst. Moreover, the analyst is there in person, so that when all goes well, the patient has someone to hate for the original failure of the facilitating environment which distorted the maturational processes.

In the particular case of this patient, very many details of infancy turned up and these could be discussed with her. Now it happens that with this particular patient I did a very rare thing in my practice. In the psychoanalysis of this peculiar case at one point I found myself with this patient on the couch and her head in my hand. Such actual contact is rare in psycholoanalytic work and I did this very naughty thing which doesn't belong to psychoanalysis at all. I tested what it would be like to just drop her head and see if her Moro Response would show up. Of course, I knew what would happen. The patient suffered very severe mental agony. This was because of her being split into two, and from there we could go on in the end to find out what was the psychological significance of the mental agony. She was able eventually to let me know what had happened to her infant self; she taught me that the circle became two circles at that moment, and the experience was an example of a split in the personality made by a specific failure of the facilitating environment, a failure of ego-augmentation.

It is very rare that I have a chance to make a test of this kind because my job as therapist is to not make these very mistakes or failures that cause intolerable mental pain. I cannot sacrifice a patient on the altar of science. But the terrible thing is that in the course of time one makes all the mistakes simply by being human, so tests get made and we deal with the results as best we can. In this one instance I made a test deliberately.

From this one detail one can see that the Moro Response

may or may not depend on the existence of a reflex arc. I am simply saying that it does not need to. There *need* not be a neurological background, or the response can be both neurophysiological and psychological. The one can change into the other. What I am suggesting is that it is not safe to ignore the psychology if one is in search of a complete statement.

There are only a few of these very primitive agonies. They include, for instance, falling for ever; all kinds of disintegration and things that disunite the psyche and the body. It will be readily seen that these are matters that concern forward movement in the emotional development that takes place if there is good enough mothering — forward movement of the emotional development of the infant. And at the same time, in terms of schizophrenia, there is backward movement. The schizophrenic has a drive to get into touch with the very processes which spoil the forward movement of the very early phase, which concerns the neonatal period. And this sort of way of looking at schizophrenia contributes both to the understanding of schizophrenia and to the understanding of infants.

There is a great deal of work to be done on the subject of birth memories and what the experience of birth means to the infant. I have no time to develop this theme here. But I want to give the dream of a schizophrenic girl who had a difficult birth. Before doing so, however, I must postulate a normal birth — that is, psychologically — in which psychological trauma is minimal. In a normal birth, from the infant's point of view, the infant brought about the birth because he or she was ready for it; and by squirming efforts or because of a need to breathe or something, the baby did something, so that from the point of view of the baby the birth is something "brought about by the baby." I think this is not only normal, but common. These felicitous events do not appear in our analytic treatments as much as they do in symbolism and in imaginative invention and in play. It is *the thing that has gone wrong* that comes up for treatment, and one of these things is delay which is infinite because there is no reason for the baby to expect an outcome.

Now I turn to the schizophrenic girl to whom I gave 2500 hours of my time. She had an exceptionally high I.Q. — about 180, I think. And she came for treatment asking me whether I would enable her to commit suicide for the right reason instead of for the wrong reason. In this I failed. When she had this dream she was at the point at which she was re-experiencing birth with all the distortions of a very intelligent grown woman. She had a highly neurotic mother, and there is evidence that she had been awakened to awareness, if such a thing is possible (as I believe it is), a few days before the birthdate because the mother suffered a severe shock. Then the birth was complicated by placenta praevia, not discovered early enough. This girl had started life on the wrong foot, and she never got into step.

In the middle of this new attempt on her part to encompass the effects of all this she borrowed my copy of Rank's *Trauma of Birth*. You see, another complication. These complications all have to be accepted in the kind of work I am reporting, and allowed for. The night after she read this book she had a dream which she felt was highly significant, and I think you will see that it was. For the analyst such dreams are daily bread. If you are used to dreams you will see how it includes a statement of her trust in me — the analyst — as the person holding her, that is to say, managing her case and doing her analysis. The dream also gives the picture of her permanent paranoid state, her vulnerability, her essential rawness against which she had organised every possible defence. A psychoanalyst here would draw attention to the fact that there are very many determinants of this dream which could not possibly have been as early as the birthdate. Nevertheless, I am giving it to you as an illustration. Here is her idea of having just been born:

She dreamed she was under a pile of gravel. Her whole body at the surface was extremely sensitive to a degree which it was hardly possible to imagine. Her skin was burned, which was her way of saying that it was extremely sensitive and vulnerable. She was burned all over. She knew that if anyone came and *did anything at all* to her, the pain would be just impossible to bear, both physical and mental. She knew of the danger that people would come and take the gravel off and do things to her in order to cure her, and the situation was intolerable. She emphasized that along with this were intolerable feelings comparable with those which belonged to her suicide attempt. (She had made two suicide attempts and afterwards she actually committed suicide.) She said: "You can't just bear anything any longer, the awfulness of having a body at all, and the mind that has just had too much. It was the entirety of it, the completeness of the job that made it so impossible. If only people would leave me alone; if only people wouldn't keep getting at me." However, what happened in the dream was that someone came and poured oil over the gravel, with her inside it. The oil came through and came on her skin and covered her. She was then left without any interference whatever for three weeks, at the end of which time the gravel could be removed without pain. There was, however, a little sore patch between her breasts, "a triangular area which the oil had not reached — from which there came something like a little penis or cord. This had to be attended to, and of course it was slightly painful but quite bearable. It simply didn't matter. Someone just pulled it off."

From this dream I think you can get (amongst the many other things) the idea of what it might feel like to have just been born. This was not one of those births that I call a normal birth because of the premature awareness that resulted from delays in the birth process.

I do know that some will find this approach unconvincing. What I have attempted to do, however, is to draw attention to work which is being done of which you might not have heard because it belongs to an alien discipline. The theory of schizophrenia as an undoing of the maturational processes of earliest infancy has much to teach the psychiatrist; also it has much, I believe, to teach the paediatrician and the neurologist and the psychologist about babies and their mothers.

[1964]

CHAPTER FIVE

The Beginning
of the Individual

IN a letter to *The Times* dated 3rd December 1966, Dr. Fisher[1] took up once more for discussion the question: when does the individual start? He was of course dealing with the Roman Catholic view that abortion is murder. The main thing in the letter was that surely it is the time of birth that is the obvious moment at which the individual starts. This is a point of view which could be shared by many but it seems to call for a statement of the various developmental stages which could be used in a discussion of this kind.

Here then is a statement which can be used and certainly it can be widened in scope. What seems to be needed is an acceptance of some degree of need for economy in the use of ideas along with the inclusion of reference to all the relevant physical and psychological phenomena.

(1) *"Conceived of."* The beginning of children is when they

---

[1] Then Archbishop of Canterbury. Eds.

are conceived of. They turn up in the play of many children of any age after 2 years. It is part of the stuff of dreams and of many occupations. After marriage there comes a time when the idea of children begins to appear. Needless to say conceiving of children does not produce them, and there is a sad example of this in Charles Lamb's "Dream Child" in the *Essays of Elia*.

(2) Conception.   This is a physical fact. Conception depends on the fertilization of an ovum and the firm lodging of the fertilized ovum in the endometrium of the uterus. There is no known case of parthenogenesis, except in mythology. In rare cases the conception occurs outside the uterus in the peritoneal cavity. The psychology of conception can be said to be of one kind or another, that is to say conceiving of has turned into conception or else conception is an accident. It is probable that we ought to associate the word *normal* with the idea of the child as a little accident and that it is senti-mental to put too much stress on the idea that the child was conceived in relation to any conscious wish. There is indeed quite a lot to be said for the little accident theory of concep-tion with the parents surprised at first, even annoyed be-cause of the immense disruption of their lives which this fact entails. It is a disaster which only turns into the opposite in favourable circumstances when the parents quickly or slowly come round to the idea that this is exactly the disaster they need.

(3) The Brain as an Organ.   The next stage must be an in-definite one and it could be split up into sub-stages. It would be logical to take the exact age at which it is dangerous for a mother to have German measles; in other words, the period somewhere about two to three months when there is very rapid growth at the inception of the changes which lead to

there being a brain. It is a very different matter to think of a child as a human being before there is a brain and to think of the child as a human being once a brain has become anatomically established. These arguments will not of course affect those who have a tremendous emotional bias towards the idea that the human being starts at the time of the fertilization of the ovum with or without its lodgement in a suitable medium. A consideration of this stage carries with it a discussion as to whether a child who is born anencephalic is a human being, and there is infinite room for disagreement in regard to the status of children with the various degrees of mental defect based on faulty development of the individual child's computer-apparatus. In practice we have no doubt that some backward children are human beings, but we may find degrees of backwardness which make us want to have a category of backwardness that puts a child outside classification as human. Tremendous emotions must be roused in any discussion on either the existence of such a borderline, or the placing of children relative to it.

(4) *Quickening*. Between (3) and (5) comes the evidence that the foetus is "alive and kicking." This which is of importance to the parents is not, however, part of the present series in that it is not constant. It is variable in its timing and it can occur along with any degree of failure of development of the brain tissue.

(5) *Viability*. At some stage or other the unborn child can be said to be viable in the sense that if born prematurely there is a chance of survival. The chance of survival depends to a very great extent on the environmental provision. Infants have been born at six months and by very careful medical and nursing care they have been brought forward even to what appears to be a normality at the time when they should

have been born. Much work has been done on the subsequent history of premature children, but for the purpose of this statement it must be taken that if one child who was born at six months has been reared to health then in theory viability is at six months, and for many this must seem to be an important stage in any discussion about the beginning of the individual.

(6) Psychology Becoming Meaningful.   At some stage or other in the development of the healthy human being there is a change which can only be described by saying that to anatomy and physiology becomes added psychology. The brain as an organ makes possible the registering of experiences and the accumulation of data and the beginnings of a sorting out of phenomena and their classification. Such words as *frustration* begin to have meaning in the sense that the infant is able to hold in the mind the idea that something was expected but the expectation was not completely fulfilled. On the basis of this kind of descriptive account one can look at the evidence for the existence of an individual person before the birth process. This must be debatable territory in any discussion, but the psychoanalyst, more than any other type of careful observer, finds himself in the position of being certain from clinical experience that the individual's psychological life is not exactly adjusted to the time of birth. The easiest way to get at this problem is to take into consideration the contrast between premature and postmature births. The psychoanalyst is forced to the conclusion that the right time for birth in the psychological sense is the full-term moment when physiologically it can also be said that the time has come for the child to leave the womb. It is even possible to formulate the idea of a normal birth, that is to say one that happens at the right moment from the infant's point of view, so that

in so far as there is any mind organization at the time the infant is able to feel the whole process as natural. It would be too complicated to take into consideration here the birth traumata of various kinds, although these also throw light on this difficult problem. It is easier to make use of the very great psychological differences that can be observed between premature and postmature infants. In brief description, the premature infant finds the incubator a natural environment whereas for the postmature infant, perhaps born with a thumb in the mouth and already frustrated, an incubator existence is exactly wrong. This theme could be developed at length, but the main conclusion is that Dr. Fisher's remark about the individual starting at birth turns out to need elaboration.

(7) Birth. This is the moment chosen by Dr. Fisher in his letter, and it perhaps refers more to the change in the mother or in the parents than to the change in the infant. Physiologically the changes brought about by birth are tremendous as is well known, but it is not necessary to think that something so momentous as the beginning of the individual is exactly linked with the birth process. Possibly this notion must be abandoned in this kind of discussion. The thing in favour of including the birth process here is the immense change that takes place in the attitude of the parents. The child might have been born dead, or might have been a monster, but here is the baby, recognised by all the world as an individual.

(8) Me–Not-me. From this point on physiology can be left to take care of itself. It includes genetic factors which determine the tendency towards maturation in the individual, and it is affected by physical disease processes which may or may not supervene. It would not be disputed that a child is an individual if encephalitis, for instance, should lead to a dis-

tortion of personality growth. The discussion is therefore now in the realm of psychology, but there are two kinds of psychology. Academic psychology, as it can be called, concerns physical phenomena. The psychology that is relevant here concerns emotional factors, the establishment of the personality, and the gradual and graduated journey from absolute dependence through relative dependence towards independence. A great deal depends on the environmental provision so that it is not possible to describe an infant or a small child without including a description of the care which is only gradually becoming separate from the individual. In other words the maturational processes facilitated in an extremely complex way by the human beings who have care of the infant reach forward towards the child's repudiation of what is not-ME and the establishment of what is ME. There comes a time when, if the infant could speak, he or she would say I AM. This stage having been reached, further progress has to be made in the firm establishment of the stage which at first alternates with renewed contact with the more primitive stage in which everything is merged or out of which the various elements have not been properly separated from each other. There is a very definite moment here in the life of every child, although it may be diffused in terms of fixed time, when the child has realised his or her own existence and has some kind of established identity not in the mind of observers but in the mind of the child. This would be a good moment to choose for talking about the beginning of the individual, but it is of course too late in any discussion of religious practice.

(9) Objectivity. Along with these changes that belong to the growth of the individual comes the capacity of the individual child gradually to allow for the fact that whereas inner

psychic reality remains personal however enriched by the perception of the environment, nevertheless there is an environment and there is a world that is external to the child that could be called actual. The difference between these two extremes is softened by the adaptation of the mother and of the parents and of the family and of those who have care of the infant and small child, but eventually the child accepts the reality principle and benefits greatly from being able to do so. All these things are a matter of growth, and they do not necessarily take place in the case of any one child who may have had a muddled environmental provision. Here again is a new stage which when reached makes for an obvious answer to the question: Is the child an individual yet?

(10) Moral Code. Interwoven with these phenomena there is the development of a personal moral code, a matter which concerns religious teachers very much. At the two extremes there are those who cannot take the risk but must plant a moral code from the beginning on the infant, and those who risk everything to enable the individual to grow a personal moral code. The up-bringing of children lies somewhere between these two extremes, but the theory of the beginning of the individual for society as well as for religious controversialists must take into account the point in time when a child feels responsible for his or her ideas and actions.

(11) Play and Cultural Experience. As a reward one might say for a satisfactory interweaving of environmental influences with the inherited maturational processes of the individual there comes about an establishment of an intermediate area which turns out to be of great importance in the individual's life. It starts with play of the intense kind that belongs only to small children and it can develop into a cultural life of infinite richness. These things, however, belong to

health, and they cannot be assumed to be a fact. In so far as they exist in the case of an individual child, so they can be said to be a vitally important part of that individual.

(12) The Personal Psychic Reality. The individual according to his or her experiences and his or her capacity to store experiences develops a capacity to believe in . . . or to trust. According to the immediate cultural provision the child will be guided towards a belief in this or that or the other, but the basis is the capacity which is based on accumulated experience both of fact and of dream. These matters although of supreme importance in a description of the individual are already too sophisticated for inclusion in a discussion on Where does the individual start? It is assumed, however, that those who are interested in the beginnings are also interested in where the individual may reach in human growth.

[1966]

CHAPTER SIX

Environmental Health in Infancy

A S we consider certain problems of infancy, you[1] bring to the issues, each in a special way, an experience of the management of infants based on their growth and development and on distortions of development due to physical factors. I wish to talk about the difficulties that do not depend on physical illness. To simplify my subject I must assume that the baby is well in a physical sense. I think you will not mind my drawing attention to the non-physical aspects of baby care since in your practice you are all the time dealing with these problems and your interest does necessarily extend outside the field of actual physical illness.

As you probably know I started off as a paediatrician and gradually changed over into being a psychoanalyst and a child psychiatrist, and the fact that I was originally a physically minded doctor has greatly influenced my work. I do

[1] Winnicott was addressing the Paediatric Section of the Royal Society of Medicine. See p. 106 Eds.

happen to have a very big volume of experience which simply arises out of the fact that I have been in active practice for forty-five years and in that time one does accumulate quite a lot of data. I can do little more here than point towards the highly complex theory of the emotional development of the human individual as a person. What I must do, however, for my own sake, is to convey some of the strength of feeling which I have accumulated in these forty-five years.

It is strange but the training of doctors and nurses on the physical side undoubtedly drains away something from their interest in infants as human beings. When I myself started I was conscious of an inability in myself to carry my natural capacity for empathy with children back to include empathy with babies. I was fully aware of this as a deficiency and it was a great relief to me when gradually I became able to feel myself into the infant-mother or infant-parent relationship. I think many who are trained on the physical side do have the same sort of block that I had myself, and they have to do a great deal of work on themselves in order to become able to stand in the baby's shoes. I am aware that this is a rather funny figure of speech since babies are not born with shoes on, but I think you will understand my meaning.

It is important for the paediatrician to know about human affairs as they are at the beginning of the life of a new individual since when they talk to parents they must be able to know about the parents' important function. The doctor comes in when there is illness, but the parents have their importance all the time, apart from illness in the child. It is a terrible complication for a mother and for parents when the doctor that they call in with such confidence if the child has pneumonia is blind to all that they do in adaptation to the baby's needs when the child has not got an illness. For example, the vast majority of difficulties in infant feeding have nothing to do with infection or with the biochemical unsuitability of the milk. They have to do with the immense problem that every mother has in adapting to the needs of a new baby. She has to do this on her own because no two babies are alike and in any case no two mothers are alike and one mother is never the same with each child. The mother cannot learn to do what is needed of her either from books or from nurses or from doctors. She may have learned a great deal from having been an infant and also from watching parents with babies and from taking part in the care of siblings, and most of all she has learned a great deal of vital importance when playing at mothers and fathers at a tender age.

It is true that some mothers are able to get help of a limited kind from books, but it must be remembered that if a mother goes to a book or to someone for advice and tries to learn what she has to do we already wonder whether she is fitted for the job. She has to know about it from a deeper level and not necessarily from that part of the mind which has words for everything. The main things that a mother does with the baby cannot be done through words. This is very obvious but it is also a very easy thing to forget. In my long experience I have had a chance to know many doctors and nurses and teachers who thought they could tell mothers what to do and who spent a lot of their time giving parents instruction, and then I have watched them when they became mothers and fathers and have had long talks with them about their difficulties, and I have found that many had to forget all they thought they knew and, in fact, had been teaching. Quite frequently they found that what they knew in this way interfered so much at the beginning that they were not able to be natural with their own first child. Gradually they managed to shed this useless layer of knowledge that is inter-twined with words and settle down to involvement with this one baby.

Holding and Handling

Infant care can be described in terms of holding, especially if one allows the meaning of the term to expand as the baby grows older and the baby's world grows more complex. Eventually the term can usefully include the function of the family unit, and in a more sophisticated way the same term may be employed to describe case-work, as practised by the caring professions.

At the beginning, however, it is the physical holding of the physical frame that provides the psychology that can be good or bad. Good holding and handling facilitates the mat-urational processes and bad holding means repeatedly inter-rupting those processes because of the baby's reactions to fail-ures of adaptation.

Facilitation, in this context, means that there is adaptation to basic need, and this happens to be something that cannot be done except by a human being. An incubator is adequate for the premature infant, but at the birthdate the baby has maturity that needs human care, even if it is valuable for the mother to be able to use a cot or a pram. The human mother can adapt to the baby's needs at this early stage because she has no other interest, for the time being.

It is the luck of most babies to be held well most of the time. On this they build confidence in a friendly world, but, more important, because of being held well enough they are able to make the grade in their very rapid emotional growth.

The basis of personality is being laid down well if the baby is held well enough. Babies do not remember being held well — what they remember is the traumatic experience of not being held well enough.

Mothers know about these things and take it all for granted. They feel physically hurt when someone, maybe the doctor doing a Moro reflex, fails to protect their baby, under their eyes, from insult.

Insult is the word that conveys the effect of bad holding on the baby, and it can be said that the majority of babies come through the early weeks or months without insult. Often, I fear it is true, the insults that do occur have been given by doctors and nurses who do not happen to be at the moment concerned as the mother is with adaptation to the basic needs of the baby.

Be sure, these insults do matter. In our work with older children and with adults we find these insults add up to a sense of insecurity as well as the other thing which is that the process of development is held up by the reactions to insult which fragment the thread of continuity that is the child.

Object-Relating

When dealing with breast or bottle feeding as paediatricians you will be thinking in terms of the physiology of breast-feeding or of bottle-feeding, and your knowledge of biochemistry has special importance here. What I am drawing your attention to is the fact that when the mother and the baby come to terms with each other in the feeding situation this is initiation of a human relationship. This sets the pattern for the child's capacity for relating to objects and to the world.

My long experience has made me see that the pattern for relating to objects is laid down in babyhood and that it does matter what happens even at the beginning. It is only too easy to think in terms of reflexes. Doctors and nurses should never fall into the trap of thinking that because reflexes are a fact they are the whole story.

The baby is a human being, immature and highly dependent, and is an individual having and storing experiences. This has immense practical importance for all concerned in the management of the earliest stages. A really high proportion of mothers could establish breast-feeding if the doctors and nurses on whom they are so dependent could accept the fact that it is only the mother who can properly perform this task. She can be hindered, and she can be helped by being given support in all other respects. She cannot be taught.

There are very subtle things that the mother knows intuitively and without any intellectual appreciation of what is happening, and which she can only arrive at by being left alone and given full responsibility in this limited area. She knows, for instance, that the basis of *feeding* is *not feeding*.

It is an insult, or shall I say a kind of rape, when an exasperated nurse pushes the mother's nipple or the nipple of the bottle into the baby's mouth and starts up a reflex. No mother left on her own would do this.

A period of time is needed for many babies before they begin to search, and when they find an object they do not necessarily want immediately to make a meal of it. They want to play round with hands and mouth, and perhaps they want to hang on with their gums. There is a wide range of variation here according to infant and mother.

This is the beginning not just of feeding; it is the beginning of object-relating. The whole relationship of this new individual to the actual world has to be based on the way things start up and the pattern that gradually develops according to the experience that belongs to this human interrelationship of baby and mother.

Here again is a huge subject, one that even concerns philosophers since the paradox has to be accepted that what the baby creates was already there, and that in fact the thing that the baby creates is part of the mother which was found.

The point is that it would not have been found had the mother not been in the special state that mothers are in when they can present themselves in such a way that they are found more or less at the right moment and in the right place. This is called adaptation to need, which enables the baby to discover the world creatively.

What can we do if we are unable to teach mothers in these matters of management? What we as doctors and nurses can do is *to avoid interfering*. It is simple really. We have to know what is our speciality and we have to know just in what way mothers do need medical and nursing care. In the knowledge of this we can very easily give to the mother just that which she alone can do.

When we are treating older children and grown-up people we find that a great deal of the disturbance which we have to deal with in terms of personality distortion turns out in the end to have been avoidable; often it has been caused by doctors and nurses or by faulty medical ideas. We repeatedly find that if a doctor or a nurse or some would-be helper had not interfered with the extremely subtle natural processes which belong to the mother-infant relationship, disturbances of development could perhaps have been prevented.

Naturally, as the baby grows a little older so life becomes more and more complex. The mother's failures at adaptation are themselves an adaptation to the child's growing need to react to frustration, to be angry, and to play about with repudiation in such a way that acceptance becomes more and more significant and exciting. Mothers and fathers, on the whole, grow up with each child in a very subtle way.

Rather quickly the baby turns into a person easily recognisable as human, but really the baby has been a human from the time of birth. The sooner we all recognise this the better.

Allow me to refer to a third area of management.

Management of Excretions

At first the baby is very much concerned with intake. This includes the discovery of objects, and the recognition of them by sight and smell and the building up of the beginnings of object constancy, by which I mean that an object gains importance in itself, not simply as one of a type, or as something that can bring satisfaction.

By the process of emotional growth and development and the maturation that corresponds with developing brain tissue the baby becomes able to take a wider view of the alimentary canal and the feeding process. Let us say that the baby in the early weeks and months has known a great deal about intake, and at the same time has been excreting faeces and urine. Intake has been complicated by all sorts of outward bound activities that have had no meaning to the baby as a person.

By the age of six or seven months the baby is demonstrably able to link excretion with intake. The baby who is rapidly growing in awareness develops an interest in the inside, that is the area that exists between mouth and anus. The same is true of the mind, so that both in mind and body the baby has become a container.

From now on there are two kinds of excretion. One is felt to be harmful, and we use the word *bad* for this, and the baby needs the mother to dispose of it. The other is felt to be good, and can be material for a gift to be given in a moment of love. Along with these feelings about function there goes the corresponding development in mind and psyche.

The reason why doctors and nurses should not interfere when parents let babies find their own way of becoming what is called "clean" or "dry" is that each baby takes time to get to the sureness of a distinction between the good and the bad stuff, and to a confidence in the proper disposal of what is to be disposed of.

The mother knows in a highly sensitive way what her baby feels about these things, because, temporarily, she is attuned to these things. She helps the baby to get rid of screaming and yelling and kicking and excretory materials, and she is ready to receive the love gifts in the moments when these are ready. She meets the baby's potential in the way that the baby has potentiality at the moment, and in the exact phase of development at which the baby happens to be at the moment.

Training makes all this subtle communication between the baby and the mother much more difficult and distorts the pattern that is being laid down for appropriate giving and for constructive effort.

Worse than interference by strict training is active and specific interference by anal and urethral manipulations and by suppositories and enemas. *These are practically never necessary* and it cannot be urged too strongly that those who care for babies be left to put into practice their respect for the babies' natural functions.

Of course there are mothers and mother-figures who cannot allow natural functions to hold sway, but these are the exceptions; at any rate we must not base our attitude on what we observe that is unnatural and ill and non-maternal.

I cannot prove these matters except to those who are prepared to give me a very great deal of time. But if you can believe me then I invite you to accept that much more important than the *treatment* of psychiatric disturbance (which has been my job) is *prophylaxis;* this can be instituted immediately, not by teaching mothers how to be mothers, but by getting doctors and nurses to understand that they *must not interfere* with the delicate mechanisms that are shown to exist in the establishment of the interpersonal relationships as between baby and mother.

CHAPTER SEVEN

The Contribution of Psychoanalysis to Midwifery

IT should be remembered that it is the midwife's skill, based on a scientific knowledge of the physical phenomena, that gives her patients the confidence in her that they need. Without this basic skill on the physical side she may study psychology in vain, because she will not be able to substitute psychological insight for knowing what to do when a placenta praevia complicates the birth process. However, given the requisite knowledge and skill, there is no doubt that the midwife can add greatly to her value by acquiring also an understanding of her patient as a human being.

Place of Psychoanalysis

How does psychoanalysis come into the subject of midwifery? In the first place, through its minute study of detail in long and arduous treatments of individual people. Psycho-analysis is beginning to throw light on all sorts of abnormality such as menorrhagia, repeated abortion, morning sickness, primary uterine inertia; and many other physical states can sometimes have as part of their cause a conflict in the unconscious emotional life of the patient. Much has been written about these psychosomatic disorders. Here, however, I am concerned with another aspect of the psychoanalytic contribution: I will try to indicate, in general terms, the effect of psychoanalytic theories on the relationships between the doctor, the nurse, and the patient, with reference to the situation of childbirth.

Psychoanalysis has already led to a very big change in emphasis which shows itself in the attitude of midwives today compared with those of twenty years ago. It is now accepted that the midwife wants to add to her essential basic skill some assessment of the patient as a person — a person who was born, was once an infant, has played at mothers and fathers, has been scared of the developments that come at puberty, has experimented with new-found adolescent urges, has taken the plunge and has married (perhaps), and has either by design or by accident fallen with child.

If the patient is in hospital she is concerned about the home to which she will return, and in any case there is the change which the birth of the baby will make to her personal life, to her relationship with her husband, and to the parents of both herself and her husband. Often, also, complications are to be expected in her relationship to her other children, and in the feelings of the children towards each other.

If we all become persons in our work, then the work becomes much more interesting and rewarding. We have, in this situation, four persons to consider, and four points of view. First there is *the woman*, who is in a very special state which is like an illness, except that it is normal. *The father*, to some extent, is in a similar state, and if he is left out the result is a great impoverishment. *The infant* at birth is already a person, and there is all the difference between good and bad management from the infant's point of view. And then *the midwife*. She is not only a technician, she is also human; she has feelings and moods, excitements and disappointments; perhaps she would like to be the mother, or the baby, or the father, or all in turn. Usually she is pleased and sometimes she feels frustrated to be the midwife.

ESSENTIALLY NATURAL PROCESS

One general idea goes right through what I have to say: that is, that there are natural processes which underlie all that is taking place; and we do good work as doctors and nurses only if we respect and facilitate these natural processes.

Mothers had babies for thousands of years before midwives appeared on the scene, and it is likely that midwives first came to deal with superstition. The modern way of dealing with superstition is the adoption of a scientific attitude, science being based on objective observation. Modern training, based on science, equips the midwife to ward off superstitious practices. What about fathers? Fathers had a definite function before doctors and the welfare state took it over: they not only felt themselves the feelings of their women, and went through some of the agony, but also they took part, warding off external and unpredictable impingements, and enabling the mother to become preoccupied, to have but one concern, the care of the baby that is there in her body or in her arms.

CHANGE IN ATTITUDE TO THE INFANT

There has been an evolution of attitude with regard to the infant. I suppose that throughout the ages parents have assumed that the infant was a person, seeing in the infant much more than was there — a little man or woman. Science at first rejected this, pointing out that the infant is not just a little adult, and for a long time infants were regarded by objective observers as scarcely human till they started to talk. Recently, however, it has been found that infants are indeed human, though appropriately infantile. Psychoanalysis has been gradually showing that even the birth process is not lost on the infant, and that there can be a normal or an abnormal birth from the infant's point of view. Possibly every detail of the birth (as felt by the infant) is recorded in the infant's mind, and normally this shows in the pleasure that people get in games that symbolize the various phenomena that the infant experienced — turning over, falling, sensations belonging to the change from being bathed in fluid to being on dry land, from being at one temperature to being forced to adjust to temperature change, from being supplied by pipeline to being dependent for air and food on personal effort.

The Healthy Mother

One of the difficulties that is encountered with regard to the midwife's attitude to the mother ranges round the problem of diagnosis. (Here I do not mean the diagnosis of the bodily state, which must be left to the nurse and the doctor, nor will I refer to bodily abnormality; I am concerned with the healthy and the unhealthy in the psychiatric sense.) Let us start with the normal end of the problem.

At the healthy extreme the patient is not a patient, but is a perfectly healthy and mature person, quite capable of making her own decisions on major matters, and perhaps more grown-up than the midwife who attends her. She happens to be in a dependent state because of her condition. Temporarily she puts herself in the nurse's hands, and to be able to do that in itself implies health and maturity. In this case the nurse respects the mother's independence for as long as possible, and even throughout the labour if the confinement is easy and normal. In the same way, she accepts the complete dependency of the many mothers who can go through the experience of childbirth only by handing over all control to the person in attendance.

RELATIONSHIP OF MOTHER, DOCTOR, AND NURSE

I suggest that it is because the healthy mother is mature or adult that she cannot hand over the controls to a nurse and a doctor whom she does not know. She gets to know them first, and this is the important thing of the period leading up to the time of the confinement. She either trusts them, in which case she will forgive them even if they make a mistake; or else she does not trust them, in which case the whole experience is spoiled for her; she fears to hand over, and attempts to manage herself, or actually fears her condition; and she will blame them for whatever goes wrong whether it is their fault or not. And rightly so, if they failed to let her get to know them.

I put first and foremost this matter of the mother and the doctor and nurse getting to know each other, and of continuity of contact, if possible, throughout the pregnancy. If this cannot be achieved, then at least there must be a very definite contact with the person who is to attend the actual confinement, well before the expected date of the confinement.

A hospital set-up which does not make it possible for a woman to know in advance who will be her doctor and her nurse at the time of the confinement is no good, even if it be the most modern, well-equipped, sterile, chromium-plated clinic in the country. It is this sort of thing that makes mothers decide to have their babies at home, with the family practitioner in charge, and with hospital facilities available only in case of serious emergency. I personally think that mothers should be fully supported in their idea when they want a home confinement, and that it would be a bad thing if in the attempt to provide ideal physical care there should come a time when the home confinement would not be practicable.

A full explanation of the process of labour and childbirth should be given to the mother by the person to whom she has given her confidence, and this goes a long way towards dispelling such frightening and incorrect information as may have come her way. It is the healthy woman who most needs this and who can make best use of the true facts.

Is it not true that when a healthy and mature woman who is in a healthy relation to her husband and family reaches the moment of childbirth, she is in need of all the immense skill that the nurse has acquired? She is in need of the nurse's presence, and of her power to help in the right way and at the right moment, should something go wrong. But all the same she is in the grip of natural forces and of a process that is as automatic as ingestion, digestion, and elimination, and the more it can be left to nature to get on with it the better it is for the woman and the baby.

One of my patients, who has had two children, and who is now gradually, so it seems, coming through a very difficult treatment in which she herself had to start again — in order to free herself from the influences on her early development of her difficult mother — wrote as follows: ". . . even allowing for the woman to be fairly emotionally mature, the whole process of labour and childbirth breaks down so many controls that one wants all the care, consideration, encouragement and familiarity of the one person looking after you, as a child needs a mother to see it through (each) one of the new and big experiences encountered in its development."

Nevertheless, with reference to the natural process of childbirth one thing can seldom be forgotten, the fact that the human infant has an absurdly big head.

The Unhealthy Mother

In contrast to the healthy, mature woman who comes under the midwife's care there is the woman who is ill, that is, emotionally immature, or not orientated to the part the woman plays in nature's comic opera; or who is perhaps depressed, anxious, suspicious, or just muddled. In such cases, the nurse must be able to make a diagnosis, and here is another reason why she needs to know her patient before she gets into the special and uncomfortable state that belongs to late pregnancy. The midwife certainly needs special training in the diagnosis of psychiatrically ill adults, so that she may be free to treat as healthy those who are healthy. Naturally the immature or otherwise unhealthy mother needs help in some special way from the person who has charge of her case: where the normal woman needs instruction, the ill one needs reassurance; the ill mother may test the nurse's tolerance and make herself a positive nuisance, and perhaps she may need to be restrained if she should become maniacal. But this is rather a matter of common sense, of meeting need with appropriate action, or studied inaction.

In the case of the healthy mother and father, the ordinary case, the midwife is the employee, and she has the satisfaction of being able to give the help that she is employed to give. In the case of the mother who is in some way ill, who is unable to be fully adult, the midwife is the nurse acting with the doctor in the management of a patient — her employer is the agency, the hospital service. It would be terrible if this adaptation to ill health should ever swamp a natural procedure adapted not to illness but to life.

Of course many patients come in between the two extremes I have devised for descriptive purposes. What I wish to emphasize is that the observation that many mothers are hysterical or fussy or self-destructive should not make midwives fail to give health its due and emotional maturity its place; should not lead them to class all their patients as childish, when in fact the majority are fully capable except in the actual matters which they must be able to leave to the nurse. For the best are healthy; it is the healthy women who are the mothers and wives (and midwives) who add richness to mere efficiency, add the positive gain to the routine that is successful merely because it is without mishap.

Management of the Mother with Her Baby

Let us now consider the management of the mother after the birth, in her first relationship to the newborn baby. How is it that when we give mothers a chance to speak freely and to remember back we so often come across a comment of the following kind? (I quote from a case description given by a colleague, but time after time I myself have been told the same.)

> He had a normal birth and his parents wanted him. Apparently he sucked well immediately after delivery but was not actually put to the breast for thirty-six hours. He was then difficult and sleepy, and for the next fortnight the feeding situation was most unsatisfactory. Mother felt that the nurses were unsympathetic, that they didn't leave her long enough with the baby. She says that they forced his mouth onto the breast, held his chin to make him suck, and pinched his nose to take him off the breast. When she had him at home she felt that she established normal breast-feeding without any difficulty.

I do not know whether nurses know that this is how women complain. Perhaps they are never in the position to hear their remarks, and of course mothers are not likely to complain to the nurse to whom they certainly owe much. Also, I must not believe that what mothers say to me gives an accurate picture. I must be prepared to find the imagination at work, as indeed it ought to be, since we are not just bundles of facts; and what our experiences feel like to us and the way they get interwoven with our dreams is all part of the total thing called life, and individual experience.

SENSITIVE POST-NATAL STATE

In our specialized psychoanalytic work we do find that the mother who has just had a baby is in a very sensitive state, and that she is very liable for a week or two to believe in the existence of a woman who is a persecutor. I believe there is a corresponding tendency that we must allow for in the midwife, who can easily at this time slip over into becoming a dominating figure. Certainly it often happens that the two things meet: a mother who feels persecuted and a monthly nurse who drives on as if actuated by fear rather than by love.

This complex state of affairs is often resolved at home by the mother's dismissal of the nurse, a painful procedure for all concerned. Worse than that is the alternative by which the nurse wins, so to speak: the mother sinks back into hopeless compliance, and the relationship between the mother and the baby fails to establish itself.

I cannot find words to express what big forces are at work at this critical point, but I can try to explain something of what is going on. There is a most curious thing happening: the mother who is perhaps physically exhausted, and perhaps incontinent, and who is dependent on the nurse and the doctor for skilled attention in many and various ways, is at the same time the one person who can properly introduce the world to the baby in a way that makes sense to the baby. She knows how to do this, not through any training and not through being clever, but just because she is the natural mother. But her natural instincts cannot evolve if she is scared, or if she does not see her baby when it is born, or if the baby is brought to her only at stated times thought by the authorities to be suitable for feeding purposes. It just does not work that way. The mother's milk does not flow like an excretion; it is a response to a stimulus, and the stimulus is the sight and smell and feel of her baby, and the sound of the baby's cry that indicates need. It is all one thing, the mother's care of her baby and the periodic feeding that develops as if it were a means of communication between the two — a song without words.

TWO OPPOSED PROPERTIES

Here then we have on the one hand a highly dependent person, the mother, and at the same time and in the same person, *the expert* in that delicate process, the initiation of breast-feeding, and in the whole bustle and fuss of infant care. It is difficult for some nurses to allow for these two opposed properties of the mother, and the result is that they try to bring about the feeding relationship as they would bring about a defecation in the case of loaded rectum. They are attempting the impossible. Very many feeding inhibitions are started in this way; or even when feeding by bottle is eventually instituted this remains a separate thing happening to the infant, and not properly joined up with the total process that is called infant care. In my work I am constantly trying to alter this sort of fault, which in some cases is actually started off in the first days and weeks by a nurse who did not see that though she is an expert in her job, her job does not include making an infant and a mother's breast become related to one another.

Besides, the midwife has feelings, as I have said, and she may find it difficult to stand and watch an infant wasting time at the breast. She feels like shoving the breast into the baby's mouth, or shoving the baby's mouth into the breast, and the baby responds by withdrawing.

There is another point: This is that, almost universally, the mother feels a little, or a lot, that she has stolen her baby from her own mother. This derives from her playing at mothers and fathers, and from her dreams that belong to the time when she was quite a little girl, and her father was her *beau ideal*. And so she may easily feel, and in some cases she *must* feel, that the nurse is the revengeful mother who has come to take the baby away. The nurse need not do anything about this, but it is very helpful if she avoids actually taking the infant away — depriving the mother of that contact which is natural — and, in fact, only presenting the infant to the mother, wrapped in a shawl, at feedtime. This last is not modern practice, but it was common practice till recently.

The dreams and imaginations and the playing that lie behind these problems remain even when the nurse acts in such a way that the mother has a chance to recover her sense of reality, which she naturally does within a few days or weeks. Very occasionally, then, the nurse must expect to be thought to be a persecuting figure, even when she is not so, and even when she is exceptionally understanding and tolerant. It is part of her job to tolerate this fact. In the end the mother will recover, usually, and will come to see the nurse as she is, as a nurse who tries to understand, but who is human and, therefore, not without a limit to her tolerance.

Another point is that the mother, especially if she be somewhat immature herself, or a bit of a deprived child in her own early history, finds it very hard to give up the nurse's care of her, and to be left alone to care for her infant in the very way that she herself needs to be treated. In this way the loss of the support of a good nurse can bring about very real difficulties in the next phase, when the mother leaves the nurse, or the nurse leaves her.

In these ways psychoanalysis, as I see it, brings to midwifery, and to all work involving human relationships, an increase in the respect that individuals feel for each other and for individual rights. Society needs technicians even in medical and nursing care, but where people and not machines are concerned the technician needs to study the way in which people live and imagine and grow on experience.

[1957]

CHAPTER EIGHT

Dependence in Child Care

I T is valuable to recognize the *fact* of dependence. Dependence is real. That babies and children cannot manage on their own is so obvious that the simple *facts* of dependence are easily lost.

It can be said that the story of the growing child is a story of absolute dependence moving steadily through lessening degrees of dependence, and groping towards independence. A mature child or adult has a kind of independence that is happily mixed in with all sorts of needs, and with love which becomes evident when loss brings about a state of grief.

Before birth the absolute dependence of the baby is thought of chiefly in physical or bodily terms. The last weeks of the baby's life in the womb affect the baby's bodily development and there is room for an idea of the beginnings of a sense of security (or of insecurity) according to the state of an unborn baby's mind, which of course is very restricted in its ability to function at this early stage because of lack of full development of the brain. Also there is a variable amount of awareness before birth and during the birth process according to the chance effects of the mother's state and of her ability to give herself over to the alarming, dangerous and usually rewarding agonies of the last stages of a pregnancy.

Because babies at the beginning of their lives are highly dependent creatures they are necessarily affected by everything that happens. They have no understanding such as we would have if similarly placed, but they are all the time having experiences which add up in their memory systems in a way either to give confidence in the world or alternatively to give lack of confidence and a sense of being like a cork on the ocean, a plaything of circumstance. In the extreme of environmental failure there is a sense of unpredictability.

The thing that ultimately builds up a sense of predictability in the baby is described in terms of the mother's adaptation to the baby's needs. This is a matter that is highly complex and difficult to describe in words, and in fact adaptation to a baby's needs can only be done well, or well enough, by a mother who has temporarily given herself over to the care of her baby. It cannot be done by trying hard or by a study of books. It belongs to the special state that most mothers find themselves in at the end of their nine-months' term, a state in which they are quite naturally orientated to this central thing, the baby, and they know what the baby is feeling like.

Some mothers do not get to this state with their first child, or they have reason to fail to get there with one child though they know they did get there with an earlier child. These things just can't be helped. No one must be expected to succeed always. And someone is usually available to supply what is needed — perhaps the child's father, or a grandmother or an aunt, when a mother cannot make it with any one baby. But on the whole this thing happens, if circumstances are fairly secure for the mother herself, and then the mother (perhaps after a few minutes or even hours of rejection of her baby) *knows* without the necessity of understanding everything how to adapt to her baby's needs. When she was a baby she had just these same needs. She does not remember but nothing of experience is ever lost, and somehow it happens that the mother meets the new baby's dependence, by a highly sensitive personal understanding that makes her able to adapt to real need.

A knowledge of theory is not at all necessary, and for millions of years mothers have been doing this job with pleasure and in a satisfactory way. Of course, if some theoretical understanding can be added to what is natural, so much the better, especially if the mother must defend her right to do well her own way, and (of course) to make mistakes. The willing helpers, including doctors and nurses who are needed for emergencies, cannot know as the mother knows (because of her nine-months' apprenticeship) what are the baby's immediate needs and how to adapt to such needs.

These needs take every possible form and they are not just periodic waves of hunger. It would be a pity to give examples lest this should seem to indicate that anyone but a poet could put into words that which has infinite variability. Nevertheless, a few points might help the reader to know what need looks like when a baby is in a state of dependence.

First, there are bodily needs. Perhaps a baby needs to be taken up and put to lie on the other side. Or a baby needs to be warmer, or less enclosed, so that water that exudes can be lost. Or the skin sensitivity needs a softer contact, wool for instance. Or there is a pain, colic perhaps, and for a few moments the baby needs to be carried round on the shoulder. Feeding has to be included in among these physical needs.

In this list protection from gross disturbance is taken for

granted — no low-flying aircraft, the baby's cot is not blown over, the sun does not come to shine directly in the baby's eyes.

Secondly, there are needs of a very subtle kind that can only be met by human contact. Perhaps the baby needs to be involved in the mother's breathing rhythm, or even to hear or feel the adult heartbeat. Or the smell of the mother or father is needed, or there is a need for sounds that indicate liveliness and life in the environment, or colours and movement, so that the baby does not become thrown back on his or her own resources, when too young or immature to take full responsibility for life.

Behind these needs lies the fact that babies are liable to the most severe anxieties that can be imagined. If left for too long (hours, minutes) without familiar and human contact they have experiences which we can only describe by such words as:

going to pieces
falling for ever
dying and dying and dying
losing all vestige of hope of the renewal of contacts.

It is an important fact that the majority of babies go through the early stages of dependence without ever having these experiences, and they do this because of the fact that their dependence is recognized and their basic needs are met, and that the mother or mother-figure adapts her way of life to these needs.

It will be appreciated that with good care these awful feelings become good experiences, adding up to a total of confidence in people and in the world. For instance, going to pieces becomes relaxation and restfulness if a baby is in good hands; falling for ever becomes the joy in being carried and the excitement and pleasure that belong to being moved; dying and dying and dying becomes a delicious awareness of being alive; loss of hope about relationships becomes, when dependence is met by constancy, a sense of assurance that even when alone the baby has someone who cares.

Most babies get good-enough care and, what is more, they get this continuously from one person, right on until they are able to be pleased to know and to trust others who feel love in this way that makes them reliable and adaptive.

On the basis of this foundation of the experience of dependence that has been met, the baby is able to begin to respond to the demands that the mother and the environment must sooner or later be able to make on the baby.

By contrast, a certain proportion of babies have experienced environmental failure while dependence was a fact, and then, in varying degrees, there is damage done, damage that can be difficult to repair. At best the baby growing into a child and an adult carries round a buried memory of a disaster that happened to the self, and much time and energy are spent in organizing life so that such pain may not be experienced again.

At worst the child's development as a person is permanently distorted so that the personality is deformed or the character warped. There are symptoms that are probably thought of as naughty, and the child must suffer from those who feel that punishment or corrective training can cure what is really a deep-seated fact of environmental failure. Or the child as a person is so disturbed that mental illness is diagnosed, and treatment is given because of an abnormality that ought to have been prevented.

The steadying element in the consideration of these very

serious matters is that in the big proportion of cases babies do not suffer in this way, and they come through without needing to spend their time and energy building a fortress around themselves to keep away an enemy that truly dwells within the fortress walls.

In the case of most babies the fact that they are wanted and loved by their mothers, and by their parents, and by the extended family, gives the setting in which each child can become an individual, not only fulfilling his or her own destiny by following the lines of hereditary endowment (in so far as external reality allows), but also happy to be able to identify with other people and with animals and things in the environment, and with society and its perpetual self-organization.

The reason why these things are usually possible is principally that dependence, absolute at first, gradually groping towards independence, was accepted as a fact and was met by human beings who adapted to the needs of the growing individual, without resentment, because of some crude sense of belonging that can conveniently be called love.

[1970]

CHAPTER NINE

*Communication Between
Infant and Mother,
and Mother and Infant,
Compared and Contrasted*

IN the first lecture of this series Dr. Sandler has been talking about the nature of psychoanalysis. In the next two
lectures you will hear about unconscious communication as
between parents and children and as between husband and
wife. Here in this lecture I am talking about communication
between infant and mother.

You will already have noted that the word *unconscious* does
not appear in my title.[1] There is an obvious reason for this.
The word *unconscious* would apply only to the mother. For
the baby there is not yet a conscious and an unconscious in
the area that I wish to examine. What is there is an armful
of anatomy and physiology, and added to this a potential for
development into a human personality. There is a general
tendency towards physical growth, and a tendency towards
development in the psychic part of the psycho-somatic partnership; there are in both the physical and the psychological

[1] See preliminary notes written for this paper, p. 107. Eds.

areas the inherited tendencies, and these inherited tendencies on the psyche side include those that lead towards integration or the attainment of wholeness. The basis for all theories about human personality development is continuity, the line of life, which presumably starts before the baby's actual birth; continuity which carries with it the idea that nothing that has been part of an individual's experience is lost or can ever be lost to that individual, even if in various complex ways it should and does become unavailable to consciousness.

If the inherited potential is to have a chance to become actual in the sense of manifesting itself in the individual's person, then the environmental provision must be adequate. It is convenient to use a phrase like "good-enough mothering" to convey an unidealized view of the maternal function; and further, it is valuable to hold in mind the concept of absolute dependence (of baby on environment), rapidly changing to relative dependence, and always travelling towards (but never reaching) independence. Independence means autonomy, the person becomes viable, as a person as well as physically (a separate unit).

This scheme of the developing human being allows for the fact that at the beginning the baby has not separated off what is not-ME from what is ME, so that in the special context of early relationships the behaviour of the environment is as much a part of the baby as is the behaviour of the baby's inherited drives towards integration and towards autonomy and object-relating, and towards a satisfactory psychosomatic partnership.[2]

[2] It surprises some people to be told that a baby's inherited tendencies are external factors, but they are as clearly external to the baby's person as is the mother's capacity to be a good-enough mother, or her tendency to become hampered in what she is doing because of a depressed mood.

The most precarious part of the complex that is called a baby is the baby's cumulative experience of life. It really does make a difference whether I am born to a bedouin where the sand is hot, or to a political prisoner in Siberia, or to a merchant's wife in England's damp but beautiful west country. I may be conventionally suburban, or illegitimate. I may be an only child, an oldest child, or the middle one of five, or the third boy of four boys in a row. All this matters and is part of me.

Like Valdar the Oft-born, an infant is born all of various ways with the same inherited potential, but from the word Go! *experiences* and gathers experiences according to the point in time and space where he or she appears. Even being born: once it was with the mother squatting, and gravity drew the baby to the centre of the world; and another time the mother was unnaturally laid out on her back, prepared as if for an operation, and she had to shove as if at stool, because gravity only pulled the baby sideways. In one birth the mother got tired of shoving, and developed uterine inertia, and so she put everything off till tomorrow morning. So she had a good sleep, but the baby, already alerted for the high dive, had to wait for ever. This had a terrible effect, and for the whole of life that person was claustrophobic and intolerant of the uncharted interval between events.

The point is perhaps made that some kind of communication takes place powerfully from the beginning of each human individual's life, and whatever the *potential* the *actual experiential* build-up that becomes a person is precarious; development can be held up or distorted at any point, and indeed may never manifest itself; in fact, dependence is at first absolute.

It will be observed that I am taking you to a place where verbalization has no meaning. What connection can there be,

then, between all this and psychoanalysis, which has been
built on the process of verbal interpretations of verbalized
thoughts and ideas?

Briefly, I would say that psychoanalysis had to start on a
basis of verbalization, and that such a method is exactly appropriate to the treatment of a patient who is not schizoid or
psychotic; that is, whose early experiences can be taken for
granted. Usually we call these patients psychoneurotic, to
make it clear that they do not come to analysis for correction
of very early experience, or for first-time early experiences
which have been missed out. Psychoneurotic patients have
already come through the early experiences well enough,
with the consequence that they have the privilege of suffering from personal inner conflicts and from the inconvenience
of the defences they have had to set up in themselves to deal
with anxiety related to the instinctual life, the chief defence
being repression. These patients are bothered by the work
they have to do keeping the repressed unconscious repressed,
and they find relief during psychoanalytic treatment in the
new simplified experiences, samples carefully chosen day by
day by themselves (not deliberately of course) for confrontation in terms of the ever-shifting transference neurosis.

By contrast, in our analytic investigations, the very early
phenomena come forward as primary features in two ways:
firstly in the schizoid phases that any patient may pass
through, or in the treatment of actually schizoid subjects
(this is not my subject here and now); and secondly in the
study of the actual early experiences of babies just about to
be born, being born, being held after birth, being cared for
and communicated with in the early weeks and months long
before verbalization has come to mean anything.

What I am trying to do here, therefore, is to look at this

one thing, the early life experience of every baby, with special reference to communication.

In terms of my hypothesis, at first there *is* absolute dependence, and the environment does indeed matter. Then how can it be that any baby comes through the complexities of the early developmental phases? It is certain that a baby cannot develop into a person if there is only a non-human environment; even the best machine could never provide what is needed. No, a human being is needed, and human beings are essentially human — which means imperfect — free from mechanical reliability. The baby's use of the non-human environment depends on the previous use of a human environment.

How then can we formulate a description of the next stage which concerns the baby's experience of life when in a state of absolute dependence?

We can postulate a state in the mother[3] — a psychiatric state, like withdrawal or concentration — this is something that (in health) characterizes her when she is getting towards the end of her pregnancy, and which lasts for some weeks or months after the event. (I have written about this, and I have given it a name — *Primary Maternal Preoccupation*.)[4]

We must assume that the babies of the world, past and present, have been and are born into a human environment that is good enough, that is, into one that is adaptive in just the right way, appropriately, according to the baby's needs.

Mothers (or mother-substitutes) seem to be able to reach this state, and it may help them if they can be told that it

[3] When I say mother I am not excluding father, but at this stage it is the maternal aspect of the father that concerns us.
[4] (1956) In *Collected Papers: Through Paediatrics to Psychoanalysis*. London: Tavistock Publications Ltd. New York: Basic Books, 1958.

only lasts a while, that they recover from it. Many women fear this state and think it will turn them into vegetables, with the consequence that they hold on to the vestiges of a career like dear life, and never give themselves over even temporarily to a total involvement.

It is likely that in this state mothers become able in a specialized way to step into the shoes of the baby — I mean — to almost lose themselves in an identification with the baby, so that they know (generically, if not specifically) what the baby needs just at this very moment. At the same time, of course, they remain themselves, and they are aware of a need for protection while they are in this state which makes them vulnerable. They assume the vulnerability of the baby. They also assume that they will be able to withdraw from this special position in the course of a few months.

So it happens that babies usually do experience optimum conditions when absolutely dependent; but it follows that a certain proportion of babies do *not*. I am saying that these babies who do not experience good enough care in this way do not fulfill themselves, even as babies. Genes are not enough.

Without pursuing this topic I must deal with one more complication that is obstructing the evolution of my argument. It concerns the essential difference between the mother and the baby.

The mother has of course herself been a baby. It is all in her somewhere, the experiential conglomerate, with herself dependent and gradually achieving autonomy. Further, she has *played* at being a baby, as well as at mothers and fathers; she has regressed to baby ways during illnesses; she has perhaps watched her mother caring for younger siblings. She may have had instruction in baby-care, and perhaps she has read books, and she may have formed her own ideas of right and wrong in baby-management. She is of course deeply affected by local custom, complying or reacting, or striking out as an independent or a pioneer.

But the baby has never been a mother. The baby has not even been a baby before. It is all *a first experience*. There are no yardsticks. Time is not measured by clocks or by sunrise and sunset so much as by the maternal heart and breathing rates, by the rise and fall of instinct tensions, and other essentially non-mechanical devices.

In describing communication between baby and mother, then, there is this essential dichotomy — the mother can shrink to infantile modes of experience, but the baby cannot blow up to adult sophistication. In this way, the mother may or may not talk to her baby; it doesn't matter, the language is not important.

Just here you will want me to say something about the inflections that characterize speech, even at its most sophisticated. An analyst is at work, as it is called, and the patient is verbalizing and the analyst is interpreting. It is not just a matter of verbal communication. The analyst feels that a trend in the patient's material that is being presented calls for verbalization. Much depends on the way the analyst uses the words, and therefore on the attitude that is at the back of the interpretation. A patient dug her nails into the skin of my hand at a moment of intense feeling. My interpretation was: "Ow!" This scarcely involved my intellectual equipment at all, and it was quite useful because it came *immediately* (not after a pause for reflection) and because it meant to the patient that my hand was alive, that it was part of me, and that I was there to be used. Or, shall I say, I can be used if I survive.

Although psychoanalysis of suitable subjects is based on verbalization, nevertheless every analyst knows that along with the content of interpretations the attitude behind the verbalization has its own importance, and that this attitude is reflected in the nuances and in the timing and in a thousand ways that compare with the infinite variety of poetry.

For instance, the non-moralistic approach, which is basic to psychotherapy and to social work, is communicated not in words, but in the non-moralistic quality in the worker. It's the positive of the music-hall song whose refrain goes: "It's not exactly what she says, it's the nasty way she says it."

In terms of baby-care, the mother who feels like it can display a moralistic attitude long before words like "wicked" make sense to the baby. She may enjoy saying: "Damn you, you little bugger" in a nice way, so that she feels better and the baby smiles back, pleased to be burbled at. Or, more subtly still, what about: "Hushabye baby on the tree tops," which isn't very nice verbally, but forms a quite sweet lullaby?

It is even possible for a mother to show her baby, who has no language yet, that she means: "God will strike you dead if you mess yourself when I've just cleaned you up," or the quite different: "You can't do that there 'ere!" which involves a direct confrontation of wills and personalities.

What then is communicated when a mother adapts to her baby's needs? I now refer to the concept of *holding*. There is a valuable economy in the use, even exploitation, of the term *holding* in description of the setting in which major communications take place at the beginning of a baby's experience of living. If I adopt this line, exploiting the concept of holding, then we have two things — the mother holding the baby, and the baby being held and rapidly going through a series of developmental phases which are of extreme importance for the establishment of the baby as a person. *The mother does not need to know what is going on in the baby.* But the baby's development cannot take place except in relation to the human reliability of the holding and the handling.[5]

We could examine the pathological or the normal, and as it is simpler to examine the normal I will adopt this one of the alternatives.

The mother's capacity to meet the changing and developing needs of this one baby enables this one baby to have a line of life, relatively unbroken; and enables this baby to experience both unintegrated or relaxed states in confidence in the holding that is actual, along with oft-repeated phases of the integration that is part of the baby's inherited growth tendency. The baby goes easily to and fro from integration to the ease of relaxed unintegration and the accumulation of these experiences becomes a pattern, and forms a basis for what the baby expects. The baby comes to believe in a reliability in the inward processes leading to integration into a unit.[6]

As development proceeds, and the baby has acquired an inside and an outside, then the environmental reliability becomes a belief, an introject based on the *experience of reliability* (human, not mechanically perfect).

Is it not true that the mother has communicated with the baby? She has said: "I am reliable — not because I am a machine, but because I know what you are needing; and I care, and I want to provide what you need. This is what I call love at this stage of your development."

[5] "The Theory of Parent-Infant Relationship." (1960) In *The Maturational Processes and the Facilitating Environment.* London: Hogarth Press and the Institute of Psychoanalysis, 1965.
[6] "Primitive Emotional Development." (1945) In *Collected Papers: Through Paediatrics to Psychoanalysis.* London: Tavistock Publications. New York: Basic Books, 1958.

But this kind of communication is silent. The baby does not hear or register the communication, only the effects of the reliability; this is registered in terms of on-going development. The baby does not know about the communication except from the effects of *failure* of reliability. This is where the difference comes in between mechanical perfection and human love. Human beings fail and fail; and in the course of ordinary care a mother is all the time mending her failures. These relative failures with immediate remedy undoubtedly add up eventually to a communication, so that the baby comes to know about success. Successful adaptation thus gives a sense of security, a feeling of having been loved. As analysts we know about this because we are all the time failing, and we expect and get anger. If we survive we get used. It is the innumerable failures followed by the sort of care that mends that build up into a communication of love, of the fact that there is a human being there who cares. Where failure is not mended within the requisite time, seconds, minutes, hours, then we use the term *deprivation*. A deprived child is one who, after knowing about failures mended, comes to experience failure unmended. It is then the lifework of the child to provoke conditions in which failures mended once more give the pattern to life.

You will understand that these thousands of relative failures of normal life are not to be compared with gross failures of adaptation — these do not produce anger because the baby is not organized yet to be angry about something — anger implies keeping in mind the ideal which has been shattered. These gross failures of holding produce in the baby *unthinkable anxiety* — the content of such anxiety is:

(1) Going to pieces.
(2) Falling for ever.

(3) Complete isolation because of there being no means for communication.

(4) Disunion of psyche and soma.

These are the fruits of *privation*, environmental failure essentially unmended.

(You will see that I have not had time to talk about communication with the intellect, even the rudimentary intellect of the baby; I must be contented with my references to the psyche half of the psycho-somatic partnership.)

It is not possible to think of *gross* adaptive failures as a form of communication. We do not need to teach a baby that things can go very wrong. If things go wrong and are not very soon mended, then the baby has been permanently affected, distorted in terms of development, and communication has broken down.

ELABORATION OF THEME

Perhaps I have said enough to draw attention to the silent early communications, in their basic form. I would say a little more by way of giving guidelines.

(*a*) The liveness of the intercommunication between mother and baby is maintained in special ways. There is the movement that belongs to the mother's breathing, and the warmth of her breath, indeed the smell of her which varies a great deal. There is also the sound of her heart-beat, a sound well-known to the baby, in so far as there is a person there to know anything before birth.

An illustration of this basic physical communicating is in the rocking movement, with the mother adapting her movements to those of the baby. Rocking insures against depersonalization or loss of the psycho-somatic partnership. Do not babies vary in their rocking rate? Is it not possible that a mother may find one baby's rocking rate too quick or too slow for natural as opposed to contrived adaptation? In describing this group of phenomena we can say that communication is in terms of mutuality in physical experience.

(*b*) Then there is playing. I do not mean fun and games, or jokes. The interplay of mother and baby gives an area that could be called common ground, shall I say a Tom Tiddler's ground, the no-man's-land that is each man's land, the place where the secret is, the potential space which may become a transitional object,[7] the symbol of trust and of union between baby and mother, a union which involves no interpenetration. So: not to forget playing, where affection and enjoyment in experience are born.

(*c*) And then there is much that could be said that has to do with the baby's use of the mother's face. It is possible to think of the mother's face as the prototype of the glass mirror. In the mother's face the baby sees him- or herself. If the mother is depressed or is preoccupied with some other ploy, then, of course, all that the baby sees is a face.[8]

(*d*) From here and from these silent communications we can go over to the ways in which the mother makes real just what the baby is ready to look for, so that she gives the baby the idea of what it is that the baby is just ready for. The baby says (wordlessly of course): "I just feel like . . ." and just then the mother comes along and turns the baby over, or she comes with the feeding apparatus and the baby becomes able to finish the sentence: ". . . a turn-over, a breast,

---

[7] "Transitional Objects and Transitional Phenomena." (1951) In *Through Paediatrics to Psychoanalysis*. London: Tavistock Publications. New York: Basic Books, 1958.
[8] "Mirror-role of Mother and Family in Child Development." (1967) In *Playing and Reality*. London: Tavistock Publications, 1971.

nipple, milk, etc., etc." We have to say that the baby created the breast, but could not have done so had not the mother come along with the breast just at that moment. The communication to the baby is: "Come at the world creatively, create the world; it is only what you create that has meaning for you." Next comes: "the world is in your control." From this initial *experience of omnipotence* the baby is able to begin to experience frustration and even to arrive one day at the other extreme from omnipotence, that is to say, having a sense of being a mere speck in a universe, in a universe that was there before the baby was conceived of and conceived by two parents who were enjoying each other. Is it not from *being God* that human beings arrive at the humility proper to human individuality?

Finally, it may be asked, to what end is all this talk about babies and mothers? I want to say that it is *not* that we need to be able to tell mothers what to do, or what to be like. If they aren't, well we can't make them. We can of course avoid interfering. But there can be a purpose in our thinking. If we can learn from mothers and babies we can begin to know what it is that schizoid patients need of us in their peculiar kind of transference, if a treatment is in progress. And there is a feedback; from schizoid patients we may learn how to look at mothers and babies and to see more clearly what is there. But *essentially* it is *from* mothers and babies that we learn about the needs of psychotic patients, or patients in psychotic phases.

It is at these early stages of intercommunication between baby and mother that the mother is laying down the basis for the baby's future mental health, and in treating mental ill-health we necessarily come across the details of early failures of facilitation. We meet the failures, but (remember!) the successes appear in terms of the personal growth that successful environmental provision made possible. For what the mother does when she does well enough is to facilitate the baby's own developmental processes, making it possible for the baby to some extent to realize inherited potential.

All we do in successful psychoanalysis is to unhitch developmental hold-ups, and to release developmental processes and the inherited tendencies of the individual patient. In a peculiar way we can actually alter the patient's past, so that a patient whose maternal environment was not good enough can change into a person who has had a good-enough facilitating environment, and whose personal growth has therefore been able to take place, though late. When this happens the analyst gets a reward that is far removed from gratitude, and is very much like that which a parent gets when a child achieves autonomy. In the context of good-enough holding and handling the new individual now comes to realize some of his or her potential. Somehow we have silently communicated reliability and the patient has responded with the growth that might have taken place in the very early stages in the context of human care.

There remains for consideration the question whether something useful can be said about the baby's communication to the mother. I am still referring to the very early stages. Certainly there is something that happens to people when they are confronted with the helplessness that is supposed to characterize a baby. It is a terrible thing to do to plant a baby on your doorstep, because your reactions to the baby's helplessness alter your life and perhaps cut across the plans you have made. This is fairly obvious but it needs some kind of restatement in terms of dependence, because although the baby is helpless in one sense, in another sense it may be said that a baby has a tremendous potential for going on living and developing and for realizing potential.

We could almost say that those who are in the position of caring for a baby are as helpless in relation to the baby's helplessness as the baby can be said to be. Perhaps there can be a battle of helplessnesses.

In making further reference to the baby's communication with the mother I suggest that this can be summed up in terms of creativeness and compliance. About this it must be said that in health the creative communication has priority over compliance. On the basis of seeing and reaching to the world creatively the baby can become able to comply without losing face. When the pattern is the other way round and compliance dominates then we think of ill-health and we see a bad basis for the development of the individual.

So in the end we can come down to the fact that the baby communicates creatively and in time becomes able to use what has been found. For most people the ultimate compliment is to be found and used, and I suppose therefore that these words could represent the communication of the baby with the mother.

I find you;

You survive what I do to you as I come to recognize you as not-me;

I use you;

I forget you;

But you remember me;

I keep forgetting you;

I lose you;

I am sad.

[1968]

ORIGINAL SOURCE OF EACH CHAPTER

🦋

1. "The Ordinary Devoted Mother." Unpublished talk given to the Nursery School Association of Great Britain and Northern Ireland, London Branch, 16 February 1966.

2. "Knowing and Learning." A BBC broadcast talk to mothers, 1950. First published in *The Child and the Family*. London: Tavistock Publications Ltd., 1957.

3. "Breast-feeding as Communication." A paper read in Winnicott's absence at a conference on breast-feeding held by the National Childbirth Trust in London, November 1968. Portions published in *Maternal and Child Care*, September 1969.

4. "The Newborn and His Mother." Lecture given at a symposium on "The Physiological, Neurological and Psychological Problems of the Neonate" in Rome, April 1964. First published under the title "The Neonate and His Mother" in *Acta Pediatrica Latina*, Vol. XVII, 1964. During the lecture the film described on page 37 was shown.

5. "The Beginning of the Individual." Written 1966 in response to

a letter to the London *Times* from Dr. Fisher, then Archbishop of Canterbury. Unpublished.

6. "Environmental Health in Infancy." In this chapter the editors have combined two versions of a lecture given at a symposium with the same title held at the Royal Society of Medicine, London, March 1967. Portions published in *Maternal and Child Care*, January 1968.

7. "The Contribution of Psychoanalysis to Midwifery." Lecture given at a course organized by the Association of Supervisors of Midwives, 1957. First published in *The Family and Individual Development*, London: Tavistock Publications Ltd., 1965.

8. "Dependence in Child Care." First published in *Your Child*, Vol. 2, 1970.

9. "Communication Between Infant and Mother, and Mother and Infant, Compared and Contrasted." Lecture in a public series about psychoanalysis, known as the Winter Lectures, Marylebone, London, January 1968. First published in *What Is Psychoanalysis?* London: Baillière, Tindall & Cassell Ltd., 1968. [D. W. W. made preliminary notes for this lecture in November 1967 which are included on pages 107–109 because they give a slightly different perspective to the subject. Eds.]

Preliminary notes for "Communication Between Infant and Mother, Mother and Infant, Compared and Contrasted." Dated November 20, 1967.

Unsatisfactoriness of current terms such as maternal instinct, symbiosis.
Limits of value of animal studies.

Contribution from psychoanalysis.
Note the word unconscious in the titles of previous lectures but not in this title.
Reason: infants not being conscious are not unconscious.
The accent is on the initial stages of development of the person who may become conscious and unconscious.
By contrast: the mother (or parent) has all the characteristics of the human mature person.
The mother has been a baby.
She has also played at being a parent and she has had ideas handed down to her.
The baby has not been a mother, nor has yet played at anything.

To get further it is necessary to make an attempt at a statement of the early stages of the development of the human baby. No time for more than a statement of:

Continuity in individual growth.
Dependence, near absolute at first.
Threat of breaks in continuity by reactions to impingements.
Impingements looked at as failures of the environment at the stage of dependence.
Gradual release of the environment due to the baby's increasing range of predicting.

Extreme example: Baby communicates by being helpless, by dependence.

There is or is not a communication according to whether the mother is or is not able to identify with the baby, to know what need is before specific needs are indicated.

This leads to a study of the changes in the mother (parent) relative to pregnancy and parenthood.
Postulate a special condition, temporary but needing abandonment as in an illness. In this condition the mother is the baby as well as herself, she does not feel a narcissistic wound when she is depleted in her own personal role by being identified with the baby.

She can be scared of this and can be helped by being told that the condition only lasts a few weeks or months, and that she will recover from it.
Without this temporary condition she cannot turn the baby's infinitely subtle needs into a communication.

The mother communicates with her baby by knowing what is needed before the need is expressed in a gesture.
From this follows naturally the gesture that expresses need, and the parent can meet this communication by appropriate response. Out of this comes deliberate communication of all kinds, not only of needs but also of wants. By this time the mother can feel free again to become herself, and to frustrate. The one state must evolve out of the other.

Frustration of "I want" produces anger. Even failure to meet deliberate "I need" gestures can produce distress, and this communication can help the mother to do what is needed, even if a little late.
By contrast, failure to meet the need that precedes deliberate gesture can only result in distortion of the infantile developmental process — nothing so good as rage can be reached.

It is to be noted that every distortion of the infantile developmental process is accompanied by unthinkable anxiety:

> disintegration
> falling for ever
> total failure of relating to objects, etc.

Our borderline cases, those that teach us to understand these things, carry round with them experiences of unthinkable anxiety, which are failures of communication at the stage of absolute dependence.

BIBLIOGRAPHICAL NOTE

THE WORKS OF D. W. WINNICOTT

Clinical Notes on Disorders of Childhood. 1931. London: William Heinemann Ltd.

The Child and the Family: First Relationships. 1957. London: Tavistock Publications Ltd.

The Child and the Outside World: Studies in Developing Relationships. 1957. London: Tavistock Publications Ltd.

Collected Papers: Through Paediatrics to Psychoanalysis. 1958. London: Tavistock Publications. New York: Basic Books, Inc., Publishers.

The Child, the Family and the Outside World. 1964. London: Penguin Books. Reading, Massachusetts: Addison-Wesley Publishing Co., Inc.

The Maturational Processes and the Facilitating Environment. 1965. London: Hogarth Press and the Institute of Psychoanalysis. New York: International Universities Press.

The Family and Individual Development. 1965. London: Tavistock Publications Ltd.

Playing and Reality. 1971. London: Tavistock Publications Ltd. New York: Basic Books.

Therapeutic Consultations in Child Psychiatry. 1971. London: Hogarth Press and the Institute of Psychoanalysis. New York: Basic Books, Inc., Publishers.

The Piggle: An Account of the Psycho-Analytical Treatment of a Little Girl. 1978. London: Hogarth Press and the Institute of Psychoanalysis. New York: International Universities Press.

Deprivation and Delinquency. 1984. London: Tavistock Publications.

Holding and Interpretation: Fragment of an Analysis. 1986. London: Hogarth Press and the Institute of Psychoanalysis.

Home Is Where We Start From. 1986. London: Penguin Books. New York: W. W. Norton & Company, Inc.

Babies and Their Mothers. 1987. Reading, Massachusetts: Addison-Wesley Publishing Co., Inc.

Selected Letters of D. W. Winnicott. 1987. Cambridge, Massachusetts: Harvard University Press.

INDEX

INDEX

Childbirth (*continued*)
  dependency of mothers during,
    73, 75
  enriched by health in the
    participants, 76
Circle
  as diagram of infant's self, 44
  becoming two instead of one, 44
Communication
  baby's use of mother's face as, 100
  baby's, to mother, 102–103
  between baby and mother through
    management of excretions, 67
  between infant and mother, xi, xii,
    89–103, 106–109
  breakdown of, through privation,
    99
  breast-feeding as, x–xi, 23–33
  deliberate, arising from needs
    being met, 108
  failure in, at stage of absolute
    dependence, 108–109
  of love, through mended failures,
    98
  of mother's reliability, 97
  silent, 97–98, 99
  taking place from the beginning of
    life, 91
  through experience of
    omnipotence, 101
  through gestures, 108
  through mutuality in physical
    experience, 99–100
  through needs of the baby, 108
  through playing, 100
Complex, the, arising out of the
    simple, 8, 65
Compliance
  in baby, and ill-health, 103
  in mother, and ill-health, 78
  vs. creativeness, 103
Conceived of, being, as beginning of
    children, 51–52
Conception
  as accident, 52

as beginning of children, 52
Confinement
  and need for mother to know those
    in attendance, 74
  home vs. hospital, 74
Continuity
  as basis for development, 90
  in care of baby, 87
  of baby, threatened by reactions to
    impingement, 107
  of being, 44, 90, 97
  of child, fragmented by reactions
    to insult, 63
  of development, 98, 107
Creativeness in baby, xii, 65, 101,
    103

De-adaptation, graduated, of
    mother, 8
Dependence
  absolute, and needs of baby, 85–86
  absolute, in the womb, 83
  absolute, of baby at the beginning,
    xi, 10, 56, 83, 90, 91, 93, 94,
    107
  and sense of security, 83
  as a fact, 83
  environmental failure during, 87,
    107, 108
  in child care, 83–88
  met by human adaptation to need,
    88
  moving towards independence, 56,
    83, 90
  of mother during childbirth, 73
  relative, 56, 83, 90
Depression, maternal, 9, 20, 90fn,
    100
Destructiveness, *see* Aggression
Determinants of Infant Behaviour,
    39
Development (*see also* Maturational
    process(es))
  and positive use of
    destructiveness, 32

INDEX

in postmature infants, 55
of 'I need' producing distress, 108
of 'I want', producing anger, 108
of infant, 8
tolerable after arrival of first
    gestures, 108

Handling
and facilitation of maturational
    processes, 62, 96–97
and psycho-somatic existence, 12
more important than actual breast-
    feeding, 25
of baby by mother, x, xii, 96–97
reliability in, 97
Health, and richness in the
    experience of childbirth, 76
Helplessness, of newborn baby, xii,
    102–103, 107
Holding
and Moro response, 63
and belief in reliability in inner
    processes, 97
and establishment of the
    personality, 96
and facilitation of maturational
    processes, 62, 96–97
and integration alternating with
    relaxation, 97
and psycho-somatic existence, 12
and warding off impingement, 20
as auxilliary ego-function, 38
as communication, 96
case-work as, 62
functioning of family unit as, 62
good enough, by mother, 38
more important than actual breast-
    feeding, 25
of baby, by doctor, 37
of baby, by mother, x, xii, 7, 16–
    17, 96
of baby, by older sister, 17–18
physical, of baby, 62
prototype of all infant care, 36–37

sensitivity to, in babies, 17, 18
Humility, arrived at from being
    God, 101

I AM
arising out of primary
    identification, 12
as stage of development, 56
Identification
of baby with mother, ix, 6–7, 11
of individual with others, 88
of individual with society, 88
of mother with baby, ix, xi, 5, 7,
    11, 36, 84–85, 107
primary, 11
Identity
and me/not-me distinction, 56
sense of, in baby, 11
Independence, in health, mixed with
    all sorts of needs, 83
Individuality
asserted by baby, 11
realised through love, 88
Infant feeding
and baby's creation of the mother,
    65
and initiation of human
    relationships, 64–65
and maternal adaptation, 64–65
difficulties in, 60–61
forced onto baby, 64
initial mismanagement of, 77
Infant(s) (see also Baby, Babies)
big head of, at birth, 75
postmaturity in, 36, 55
prematurity in, 36, 53, 54, 55
seen as human from birth, 72
Inherited tendencies (see also
    Maturational Processes)
actualisation of, and adequate
    environment, 90, 101–102
as external to the baby, 90fn
not enough by themselves for self
    fulfillment, 94

119

INDEX

Menstruation, xi

Mental defect, 53

Merging, of infant with
environment, 56

Midwife

and attitude towards mother, xi

and establishment of feeding, 79

and importance of knowledge and
skill, 69, 74

and management of ill patients,
75–76

and management of mother and
baby, 76–81

and need to give health its due,
76

and need to know her patient, 75

and need to make psychiatric
diagnosis, 72–73, 75

and practice of taking the baby
away, 80

as a person with human feelings,
71, 79, 80

as employee, 76

as persecutory figure, 78, 80

mother's trust in, xi, 69, 73

Midwifery, and psychoanalysis, xi,
69–81

Mirror, mother's face as, 100

Moral code

development of, as beginning of
individual, 57

personal vs. implanted, 57

Morley, Robert, 5

Moro response, the

an example of not good enough
mothering, 42–43

and premature awareness in
infant, 43, 44

as example of bad holding, 63

as insult to baby, 63

elicited in regressed woman
patient, 45

psychology of, 45–46

reaction of baby to, 42–43

Mother(s)

adaptation of, to baby, xii, 6–7,
18, 64–65, 84, 85, 86, 97, 100–
101

and acting naturally, 7, 16, 18, 78

and belief in a persecuting
woman, 77–78

and change in personal life at birth
of baby, 5–6, 70, 107

and experience of being a baby, xi,
6, 30, 70, 94, 107

and facilitation of experience of
omnipotence, 100–101

and fear of total preoccupation
with baby, 93–94, 108

and foundation for mental health
of child, 19, 24–25, 101

and giving birth, 91

and graduated failures in
adaptation, 8, 65

and handling of baby, x, xii, 18–
19, 97

and holding of baby, x, xii, 17–19,
63, 96–97

and importance of previous life
experience, 6, 30–31, 61, 70,
79–80, 94, 107

and intuitive knowledge about
feeding babies, 64

and intuitive knowledge of baby's
needs, 85–86, 108

and loss of care of midwife, 80

and love expressed as reliability,
97

and need for continuity of care in
childbirth, 75

and need for explanation about
labour, 74

and need for protection while
vulnerable, 94

and need for space to care for
baby, 19, 26

and physical contact with baby,
86, 99

INDEX

Object
-constancy, 66
discovery of, and intake, 66
protection of, by baby, 31
survival of, xi, 32
Object-presenting, 38, 78
Object-relating, 63–66
and symbolic use of objects, 13
inherited drives towards, 90
not absolutely dependent on
breast-feeding, 25–26
pattern of, set through infant
feeding, 65
task in primitive emotional
development, 38
Objectivity, achievement of, as
beginning of child, 56–57
Omnipotence, baby's experience of,
xii, 8, 101
Oneness, feeling of, between baby
and mother, 7, 11
Ordinary devoted mother, the, ix, 3–
14
origin of the phrase, 3–4
positive value of, 9

Paradox, of creating what is found,
65
Paranoid state, in schizophrenic
patient, 47
Parents
and change in attitude at birth of
baby, 55, 107
and growing up with children, 65
and need to insist on self-
fulfillment, 27
importance of full-time function
of, 60–61
rewarded when children achieve
autonomy, 102
Patient(s) (*see also* Case material)
and need for regression in
analysis, 44–45

schizoid, and infant-mother
relationship, 101
Personality
basis of, laid down by holding, 62
development of, and continuity of
line of life, 90
development of, and holding, 96–
97
distortion of, through
environmental failure, 87
distortion of, through physical
disease, 55–56
richness in, and breast-feeding,
24, 29
richness in, and good-enough
mothering, 25
split in, owing to faulty holding,
44
Play(ing)
and conceiving of children, 52
and cultural activity, 57
at mothers and fathers, 61, 70, 79–
80, 94, 107
common ground between baby
and mother, xii, 100
early good experiences recreated
in, 46–47
games that symbolise birth, 42, 72
intense, in small children, 57
intermediate area of, 57, 100
origins of affection and enjoyment
in, 100
vitally important to individual, 58
Poet who stayed in bed, 5–6
Pregnancy
as period of preparation, 5
new, too soon after first baby, 8
Premature awareness, owing to
environmental failure, 43, 44,
49
Preoccupation (*see also* Adaptation,
Identification, Mother(s))
mother's fear of state of, 93–94,
108

D. W. WINNICOTT

1896–1971

Dr. Winnicott began his medical career in paediatrics and kept an interest in the physiological side of paediatrics while becoming more and more involved in the study of child psychology. His contributions to our understanding of human development, based on extensive clinical work with mothers, babies, and young children, are internationally known and valued.

Dr. Winnicott began his medical studies at Jesus College, Cambridge, and after a period of war service continued them at St. Bartholomew's Hospital in London. Apart from his year as a resident at St. Bartholomew's, his hospital appointments were all at children's hospitals. Dr. Winnicott practiced and taught child psychiatry and psychoanalysis for over forty years and was elected President of the British Psycho-Analytical Society. He was a prolific contributor to psychoanalytic and medical journals and lectured widely on child development to many groups of professionals in this field: teachers, midwives, parents, social workers, magistrates, and physicians as well as to psychoanalysts and psychiatrists. Among his best known books are *Through Paediatrics to Psychoanalysis*, *The Child, The Family and The Outside World* and *Playing and Reality*.

CLASSICS IN CHILD DEVELOPMENT

also in this series

THE BIOGRAPHY OF A BABY
by Milicent Washburn Shinn
Introduction by T. Berry Brazelton, M.D.

THE CONTINUUM CONCEPT
by Jean Liedloff

THE CHILD, THE FAMILY, AND THE OUTSIDE WORLD
by D.W. Winnicott
Introduction by Marshall H. Klaus, M.D.